SELF-CONFIDENCE WORKBOOK

YOU NEED TO TRUST YOURSELF

Discover the Keys To Increase Your Self-Esteem and Confidence While Overcoming Social Anxiety With Effective Communication Skills

JOHN TAYLOR

Copyright © 2020 John Taylor

All Rights Reserved

Copyright 2020 By John Taylor - All rights reserved.

The following book is produced below with the goal of providing information that is as accurate and reliable as possible. Regardless, purchasing this eBook can be seen as consent to the fact that both the publisher and the author of this book are in no way experts on the topics discussed within and that any recommendations or suggestions that are made herein are for entertainment purposes only. Professionals should be consulted as needed prior to undertaking any of the action endorsed herein.

This declaration is deemed fair and valid by both the American Bar Association and the Committee of Publishers Association and is legally binding throughout the United States.

Furthermore, the transmission, duplication or reproduction of any of the following work including specific information will be considered an illegal act irrespective of if it is done electronically or in print. This extends to creating a secondary or tertiary copy of the work or a recorded copy and is only allowed with express written consent from the Publisher. All additional right reserved.

The information in the following pages is broadly considered to be a truthful and accurate account of facts and as such any inattention, use or misuse of the information in question by the reader will render any resulting actions solely under their purview. There are no scenarios in which the publisher or the original author of this work can be in any fashion deemed liable for any hardship or damages that may befall them after undertaking information described herein.

Additionally, the information in the following pages is intended only for informational purposes and should thus be thought of as universal. As befitting its nature, it is presented without assurance regarding its prolonged validity or interim quality. Trademarks that are mentioned are done without written consent and can in no way be considered an endorsement from the trademark holder.

Table of Contents

PART I 12

Chapter 1: Self-Confidence In Various Situations 13

    How a Lack of Self-Confidence Affects Us 14

Chapter 2: Social Anxiety 16

    Social Anxiety and Lack of Confidence In Specific Situations 17

Chapter 3: Learning to Become Comfortable 22

    Building Your Self-Confidence 22

        Groom Yourself Regularly 23

        Photoshop Your Self-Image 23

        Destroy Negative Thoughts 23

        Get to Know Yourself 24

        Be Kind and Generous 24

        Be Prepared 24

        Know Your Principles and Live By Them 25

        Speak Slowly 25

        Stand Up Straight 26

        Increase Your Competence Levels 26

        Set Small Goals and Achieve Them 26

        Change Small Habits About Yourself 26

        Focus Your Attention on Solutions 27

        Become Active 27

        Gain More Knowledge 27

    Overcoming Procrastination 28

    Build Confidence At Work 30

Chapter 4: Getting Rid of Social Anxiety..33

PART II 38

Chapter 1: Self-Esteem and Valuing Yourself 39

    How Low Self-Esteem Is Developed 41

        The Different Types of Parents 41

        Bullying..42

        Trauma 44

        The Science of Self-Esteem 46

Chapter 2: How You Can Matter to Yourself 48

    How to Build Self-Awareness..49

        Recognize What Bothers You About Other People 49

        Meditate on Your Mind 50

        Draw a Timeline of Your Life 51

        Identify Your Emotional Kryptonite..51

        Travel and Get Out a Little Bit 52

        Pick Up a New Skill...52

        Clarify Your True Values 53

Chapter 3: Creating a Stronger Self 55

    Managing Your Ego 55

        Don't Take Things Personally 56

        Accepts All of Your Mistakes 56

        Stop Being Self-Conscious 56

        Realize That Your Ego Will Never Go Away 58

        You Are Not the Best...58

        Imagine Your Ego as Another Person 58

        Stop Bragging...59

Be Grateful for the Little Things 59

Learn to Compliment Others 59

Forgiving People 60

Overcoming Trauma 63

Chapter 4: Changing Our Minds 66

How To Ignore Things 66

Stop Comparing Yourself To Others 66

Ignore Societal Pressure 67

Start Living In The Present Moment 68

Leverage Your Purpose 68

The Mindset Shift 69

Now That Your Self-Esteem is High 70

Chapter 1- What is Self Compassion 73

The Three Elements of Self-Compassion 74

Discovering Self Compassion 75

Conclusion 76

Chapter 2- Benefits of Self-Compassion 78

Self-Compassion At Work 79

Self-Compassion In Relationships 80

Self-Compassion In Life 81

Chapter 3: Myths about Self Compassion 83

#1 Self-Compassion is just a person crying out for self-pity 83

#2 Self-compassion is a sign of weakness 84

#3 Self-Compassion can make you a complacent person 85

#5 Self-compassion makes us selfish 87

Conclusion 89

Chapter 4- Dealing with Negativity 90

What Can Negative Thinking do to your Brain? 90

What Can Positive Thinking do to your Brain? 91

Steps to deal with Negative thoughts and Events...............................93

Learn to Forgive Yourself 95

Steps to Overcome Failure..97

Surrounding yourself with Positive People...99

Your GOOD Category 99

Think About How You Interact with People......................................100

Benefits of surrounding yourself with Positive People 101

Chapter 5: Building and Mastering Emotions 103

The Five Categories of Emotional Intelligence (EQ) 103

Self-regulation includes: 104

Motivation is made up of: 104

Creating a Balance with Emotional Awareness.................................106

Conclusion...109

Chapter 6: Practical steps for Becoming self compassionate..................110

Practicing Creative Visualization to Encourage Self-Compassion 114

Concise Guidelines for Creative Visualization: 117

Using Affirmations...118

Making Affirmations Work for You 120

Examples of Positive Affirmation 121

Mindfulness Meditation for Self-Compassion 122

Exercise 1 – Mindful Breathing 122

Exercise 2 – Awareness...123

Exercise 3 – Mental Focus...125

Chapter 1: What is Holding You Back 127

Why People Procrastinatn 127
Abstract Goals 129
Not Having Foreseeable Rewards.. 130
A Disconnect from Our Future Selves.................................. 131
Being Too Optimistic 131
Being Indecisive 132
Task Aversion 133
Perfectionism.. 133
Self-Handicapping.. 134
Other Major Reasons for Not Getting Things Done 135
Not Sure What to do 135
There is No Deadline or Accountability............................. 135
Don't See Any Consequences 136
Why Getting Things Done is Critical... 137
Chapter 2: It's Time to Get Things Done 139
Overcoming Procrastination... 139
Don't Catastrophize 139
Focus on Your "Why"... 140
Get Out Your Scheduler... 141
Be Realistic... 141
Break it Down.. 142
Stop With the Excuses.. 142
Find an Accountability Partner... 142
Optimize Your Environment... 143
Forgive Yourself 143
Mindfulness Meditation Technique 144
Body Scan Meditation.. 144

- Sitting Meditation 144
- Walking Meditation 145
- Simple Mindfulness 145
- 15 Habits of Highly Productive People 146

Chapter 3: Visualizing a Better Future 149

- How to Visualize Your Future 149
- More Tips for Visualization 150
  - Visualize Your New Life 150
  - Create a Vision Board 151
  - Write Down Your goals 151
  - Let Yourself Zone Out 151
  - Say Your Goals Out Loud 152
  - Think About What You Want and not What You Don't Want 152
- Life When You Get Things Done 152
  - A Feeling of Relaxed Control 153
  - Your Thinking Will Be Stimulated 153
  - More Organization and Less Clutter 153
  - Less Time for Worry 154

Chapter 1: Is This for You? 156

Chapter 2: Your Toolbox, DBT 158

Chapter 3: Finding Yourself through Mindfulness 163

Chapter 4: Taking Mindfulness to the Next Level with Advanced Meditation Techniques 167

Chapter 5: Using Your New Tools to Process Negative Emotions 172

Chapter 6: Defining Your Goals, Your Values, and Yourself 176

Chapter 7: Living in the Positive! 179

Chapter 8: How DBT Has Enhanced Your Life 183

PART I

Chapter 1: Self-Confidence In Various Situations

"Each time we face our fear, we gain strength, courage, and confidence in the doing."

-Theodore Roosevelt

While we have been speaking of self-worth and self-value, the focus of this chapter will be self-confidence, which is a different subject altogether.

Self-confidence is when you have faith in yourself and your abilities in a particular situation, and it does not relate to overall self-worth. If your self-confidence levels are low, it is because you are not comfortable in a particular setting, for whatever reason.

To help make self-confidence more clear, here are a few scenarios that showcase it in different circumstances.

- A doctor is self-confident when he performs any type of procedure within his specialty. He has so much training and experience that he truly believes in his skills and abilities to perform in various situations at work. When this same doctor goes for a hike, he does not have the same level of confidence in conquering a high peak, because he is out of shape.

- A mechanic can fix any car with his eyes closed. He has been a mechanic for so many years, that he is confident there is nothing that will come into his garage that he cannot handle. When this mechanic tries to work on the plumbing in his home, he is not very successful and has no confidence in his ability to perform the tasks.

- A great artist is confident in his ability to paint a portrait. If you ask him to solve a math problem, he has no confidence whatsoever.

These examples showcase how self-confidence can truly be based on the state of affairs, depending on what a person is facing at the moment. To handle a situation well, you must have self-confidence in your ability to do so. Self-confidence is gained through training, education, repetition, and life experience. It is impossible to be confident in every situation you ever come across, but the more you are willing to learn, the more confidence you will gain throughout life.

How a Lack of Self-Confidence Affects Us

As I mentioned before, self-confidence is circumstantial and will impact various areas of your life differently. Depending on how much experience, knowledge, or training, we have in different aspects of life, our confidence will ebb and flow. The key is to have self-confidence in the important areas of our lives, where it really matters. There are many examples in our everyday lives where self-confidence will play a major role.

Regarding the work setting, people who lack confidence in this arena cannot perform their necessary duties at an adequate level. This means poor job performance, being overlooked for raises and promotions, and even being let go from a position. If a person performs their job well, low self-confidence can still impact their desire to move up the latter. If they are confident in their particular position but do not feel confident at a higher level, like management, then they won't go after the promotion. They will simply stay put, even though they have the potential to do more.

Concerning starting a business, a certain level of confidence is needed to perform numerous tasks. There are many independent skills involved in running a business, and chances are, you will be doing most of them yourself when you first start. You need to have the proper training and education in these different areas, like finance, setting a budget, and marketing, etc., or you will not succeed in them. If you feel you can't do them yourself, then you may have to higher someone to do so. It may be worth it to avoid errors.

Self-confidence matters in our personal lives too. In order to find friends or develop relationships, we must have confidence in our abilities to form them. For example, it takes a lot of confidence for a man to walk up to a woman and say, "hi." To make friends, you must have the courage to talk to people. To learn new things and experience a new adventure, you must also have confidence in yourself to perform them. Once again, confidence comes from experience, and the more you put yourself out there, the more confident you will become.

Confidence is crucial in specific social settings. For example, during a work meeting, a lack of confidence can hold you back from speaking up, even if you have something very important to say. You won't get the necessary information out there that many people in the meeting could receive value from. This also relates to socializing with friends. You may have a friend who is harming themselves, but because you are uncertain how they will react, you ca nothing. You do not have the confidence that you will be able to respond appropriately.

A lack of confidence does not allow you to communicate assertively, which is important in order to get what you want. Instead of asking for things directly, you will beat around the bush and hope that the person will pick up on your clues. You will also use minimizing language, like "Sort of" or "kind of." This type of communication makes it seem like you lack conviction, and no one will take you seriously. You will just appear weak. Being assertive is essential, whether you are asking for something at working or setting boundaries with your friends.

If you suffer from low self-confidence, then every aspect of your life will suffer. We will get into different ways of increasing your confidence in the next chapter. For now, we will discuss how self-confidence works in different settings, especially in those that create anxiety for everybody.

Chapter 2: Social Anxiety

For this chapter, I will provide more detail for a specific type of confidence issue, and that is social anxiety.

Social Anxiety and Lack of Confidence In Specific Situations

Social anxiety is an actual disorder where a person has a phobia in which a person feels like they are being watched and judged by everybody. There may be select situations where this is actually happening, but in most circumstances, it is an unfound fear. This is an extreme situation where a person has a lack of confidence in everything they do, and therefore, feel like they are the center of attention.

Going for a job interview, taking a test, going on a date, or speaking in public are normal things that create anxiety in almost everybody. It is amplified greatly in someone who has a social anxiety disorder. Furthermore, these individuals actually become nervous during normal, everyday activities like shopping for food, parking their car, or using a public restroom. Their anxiety is so intense that they feel judged in every moment of their lives. This fear can become so strong that it interferes with people going to work, attending school, talking to their friends, or doing any other menial task during the day.

It is estimated that about seven percent of the American population suffers from social anxiety. While this number is not massive, it shows that the problem is not uncommon.

Researchers believe there is a genetic component where areas of the brain that deal with fear and anxiety are involved. However, there is no explanation as to why some family members are affected while others are not. For example, out of two siblings, one may be shy and quiet, while the other one is loud and bombastic.

Another cause of social anxiety may be underdeveloped social skills. Some individuals will feel discouraged after talking to people, even if the conversation did not go poorly, which will cause them to avoid interactions in the future. The lack of interaction will just lead to further underdeveloped social skills, and the social anxiety trend will continue.

Many people with this disorder do not have anxiety in specific social settings, but instead in areas where performance is involved. This is often referred to as performance anxiety and is related to performing in front of a crowd in any type of capacity, whether it is a speech, dance recital, or sporting event. Speaking in public is one of the worst fears that people have, and in some surveys, it is number one. Jerry Seinfeld used to make the joke that during a funeral, most people would rather be inside the casket than the ones giving the eulogy.

Even if a person is confident in the subject matter, having to discuss it in a large crowd, with hundreds, or even thousands, of eyes, looking at them, will create a high level of anxiety. This situation would be unsettling for many people. There are many reasons why someone would have a fear of speaking in public, and it goes beyond just being nervous.

Fear and anxiety will create a physiological response within us. During this process, our autonomic nervous system, which works as a protective mechanism by keeping us alert, will make us hyper-arousable. Generally, this is done to put the body in a state of battle. As a result, we will have an emotional experience to fear, which will interfere with our ability to perform well in front of an audience.

Another factor to consider is the person's beliefs about the speaking engagement. Many people will feel that if they screw up something in front of a crowd, it will hurt their credibility, and therefore, their careers. They also feel that their performance will never be forgotten, and their whole public image will be destroyed in an instant. The fact that everyone has a camera on their phones lends some more credibility to this fear. These feelings cause people to overthink and become extremely anxious beyond their control.

Anxiety during a public speech is greater in those who don't do it often. The more a person speaks in front of a crowd, the less nervous they become over time. Unfortunately, most people do not speak in front of audiences constantly, unless they do it for a living. If someone only speaks a few times a year or less, then they will usually have anxiety every time. Also, a person's status in relation to the audience members can play a role in their confidence levels. For example, if a person is speaking in front of high-level executives about a topic they already know, then this can create an immense amount of fear. They worry about having their speech dissected. What a person must realize here is that it is not so much the content of the speech, but how it is presented.

The most obvious reason for the fear of public speaking is the actual skill involved. Speaking in front of an audience involves getting the people engaged.

This is done by proper timing, eye contact, stage presences, charisma, and a little bit of humor. The bottom line is, you must be able to connect with the audience somehow, or they will not care whatsoever what you have to say, no matter who you are. Your status may capture their attention for a while, but if you can't keep their attention, your speech will be forgotten before it even starts. Many people know this and are worried that they won't be able to hold their audience's attention.

The more anxious you are, the less likely you are to perform well. It is to your advantage to be as relaxed as possible and overcome your social anxiety, which is much easier said than done.

Aside from public speaking, another social situation that can cause anxiety is being in a large crowd. Many people with social anxiety are okay when they are just around their friends. However, once the circle starts increasing, their anxiety grows tremendously. This type of fear is known as enochlophobia, and it is related to the perceived dangers posed by large gatherings of people you may see in everyday life. The fear includes getting lost, stuck, or harmed in some manner by the crowd.

Most of you are probably thinking of concerts or other places where organized gatherings occur. The simple solution here would be to avoid these types of events. However, this fear also encompasses busy metropolitan areas, public transits like the bus or subway, or even workspaces with a lot of employees. Any type of space where a large number of people are, a person with this type of phobia will become fearful and anxious.

In the next chapter, we will describe various ways to build up your self-confidence, so you can be prepared to handle any situation, even if you are not familiar with it.

Chapter 3: Learning to Become Comfortable

When you lack self-confidence, it means you are unsure of yourself in a particular setting. You have a certain level of discomfort, which precludes you from going all-in when performing a certain task. Unfortunately, if your confidence levels are not high enough, then you will not perform at your highest level. This does not mean you aren't nervous or slightly anxious. It literally means that you do not believe in yourself in a specific situation.

A person will never feel fully confident in every aspect of life. There will be plenty of times when we are faced with something new, and it will completely throw us off our game. The goal of this chapter will be to build self-esteem in some of the most important areas of our lives and also develop the critical thinking skills we need to overcome almost any situation, no matter how unfamiliar it may be.

Building Your Self-Confidence

Nobody is born with an unlimited amount of self-confidence. Also, people are not born with zero confidence. It is something that either gets built-up or deteriorated over time. Unfortunately, many people have had their confidence shattered so many times that they never have confidence in themselves in any situation, no matter how familiar they are with it. The practices in this section will focus on building self-confidence in the general sense, so you are ready to attack life, no matter what gets thrown your way.

Groom Yourself Regularly

This may sound obvious, but many people do not realize how good they will feel when they take the time to shower, do their hair, clean their nails, and dress nicely. The old saying, "When you look good, you feel good," Holds a lot of truth. Even if you have nothing important planned for the day, take the time to groom yourself. You will automatically feel more confident in any situation you come across. You don't have to go to the salon every day or wear thousand-dollar suits. The goal is to look good when you observe yourself in the mirror. This could mean wearing your favorite shirt and jeans combination.

Photoshop Your Self-Image

We take a lot of stock in our self-image. No matter how much we try to say that looks don't matter, we like to look at ourselves in the mirror and see a positive self-image. You can alter your self-image by mentally photoshopping yourself in a way that is positive to you. You can then work on obtaining this image in real-life. For example, if you see yourself 20 pounds lighter, then keep this image in your mind and work towards it.

Destroy Negative Thoughts

No matter how unfamiliar you are with a situation, you are more likely to handle it well if you get rid of your negative thoughts. These simply take up space in your mind and have no value in your productivity. Be aware of our self-talk and how you think about yourself. This may sound ridiculous, but when you find a negative thought entering your mind, picture it as an object or creature that you want to destroy. For example, when you begin having negative thoughts, picture them as bugs. Now, squash those bugs mentally, and you will effectively destroy your negative thoughts. This is a great mental trick to play on yourself. After getting rid of the negative thought, replace it with a positive one.

Get to Know Yourself

When going into battle, it is best to know your enemy very well, no matter who they are. When you are dealing with low self-confidence, your enemy becomes yourself. This is why it is important to get to know yourself as well as you can. Listen intently to your thoughts, write about yourself in a journal, determine what thoughts about yourself dominate your mind, and analyze why you have negative thoughts.

Next, write down all of the positive aspects that you have, no matter how minuscule they may seem. Start thinking about the limitations you have and determine if they are real and verified, or just something you came up with in your head. Dig as deep you can get into your psyche, and you will find out more about yourself than you had ever known. The more you know about yourself, the greater self-confidence you will have.

Be Kind and Generous

Be kind and generous to others, whether it is time, money, or other resources, will be great for improving your self-image. When you are genuinely able to help someone when they need you, then it makes you feel good about who you are. It gives you a sense of purpose.

Be Prepared

Be as prepared for life as you can. Think about this for a moment: if you are taking an exam, and have not studied, then you won't be prepared, and your confidence level will be very low. On the other hand, if you did study intensely, then you will be much more prepared and have a greater amount of confidence. Imagine life as one big exam. The more prepared you are every day, the more confident you will feel in any situation. The following are some general ways you can be more prepared.

- Have plenty of food in the refrigerator and cabinets.
- Have a substantial emergency fund.
- Have the basics as far as emergency supplies at all times.
- If you have something specific planned for that day, like a presentation or meeting, be as prepared as possible for it.
- Always be on alert for dangerous situations.

Know Your Principles and Live By Them

What are the main principles upon which your life is built? If you are not sure, then it's time to sit down and really think about it. Otherwise, your life will be completely directionless. When you know your principles and live by them, then you are truly living your passion, and this is great for your self-confidence. People who are simply coasting through life with no real values will have no goals in life either. They are simply existing and not fully living. When you refuse to live your life based on your values, then you lack confidence in yourself.

Speak Slowly

Speaking slowly will make a huge difference in how people perceive you. It shows a sense of knowledge and confidence in what is being said. Someone who speaks with a rapid-fire approach generally does so because they are not confident in what they are saying. They just want to get the word out there and hope nobody calls them out. Even if you don't feel totally confident on a subject, try speaking slowly anyway, and see how much your self-confidence actually builds. This can be a great mind trick. When you speak slow, you have more time to formulate good thoughts. Of course, I am not telling you to take it to the extreme here, just don't spit words out like a machine gun.

Stand Up Straight

This is another simple trick to help you feel better about yourself. When you slouch, not only does it showcase a lack of confidence, you actually have less self-confidence. This goes along the lines of looking good and feeling good. And trust me, when you stand up straighter, you will look much better.

Increase Your Competence Levels

Simply put, if you are more competent in something, you feel more confident. You gain competence through practice and training. In any situation in life, get as much training as you can to feel as fully self-confident as you can. Let's use the example of a house fire. I hope that your house never burns down, but if it does, I want you to feel confident that you and your family can escape safely. Map out an escape plan and practice it as often as you can. Many companies do quarterly evacuation drills. Employ this same practice in your house. If an emergency like this ever occurs, you will have more competence, and therefore, confidence in being able to handle it. Think of as many possible circumstances as you can in life, and determine ways to practice and train in them.

Set Small Goals and Achieve Them

When you are able to achieve a goal in life, it is a huge boost to your confidence. Set small goals regularly and then work hard to accomplish them. Remember, they should be small and reasonable. You can even cut down larger goals into smaller achievable steps. For example, if your goal is to buy a car, you can create a goal to save a certain amount of money by the end of the month, and then every month after that.

Change Small Habits About Yourself

Trying to change a large habit all at once can be very difficult, and the chances of failure are high. This will be a huge shot to your confidence. Instead, focus on smaller habits that will lead to big change. For example, if your goal is to wake up early and workout before starting your day, then don't try to wake up two hours earlier on the first day. Start by waking up 10-20 minutes early until it becomes a habit, and then increase the time from there as you feel comfortable.

Focus Your Attention on Solutions

So often, we are completely focused on the problems and pay no attention to the solutions. For example, you may always complain about being tired, but do nothing to change it, because the solutions never enter your mind. Make it a habit to focus on solutions whenever a problem enters your mind. You will get more accomplished and gain a lot of self-confidence. For example, if you are tired every day, then what is making you that way. Are you not sleeping enough? If not, then why is that? Are you eating too much sugar before going to bed? Do you have a poor diet during the day? Are you drinking enough water? See how man questions you can get answered if you just shift your focus from the problems to the solutions. Try it out with any small problems that you may have and notice the results.

Become Active

You may have noticed that when you start taking action, work starts getting done. So often, people sit around and worry about how they will get something done, rather than doing the work to get it done. Excessive worry leads to a lack of confidence. The more you worry, the lower your self-confidence will become. If you take action, you will obtain results. Results lead to increased confidence. Next time you find yourself worrying about something, start developing a plan and execute it. Hours of taking actions will give you better results than hours of sitting around and worrying.

Gain More Knowledge

Empowering yourself with knowledge is one of the greatest ways to build self-confidence. You will never know everything, but the more you know, the better you will feel about yourself. This goes along the same vein as building competence. You become more knowledgeable on a subject by studying and practicing it. This does not have to be something you will use. It can just be for your own self-fulfillment. According to psychology, one of the biggest reasons for low self-confidence is either misinformation or a lack of information. As you become more empowered with knowledge, you will gain more information too.

Just like with the steps to gain self-esteem, these previous steps must be employed regularly. Our self-confidence will be challenged all the time, so it is in our best interest to build it up regularly through practice and discipline. Think of your confidence as a muscle that you must work out every single day. Do this, and you will be amazed at how much self-confidence you have throughout your life.

Overcoming Procrastination

People love to procrastinate. And why wouldn't they? Why do something now if you can do it tomorrow? I'll tell you why. What keeps you from making the same excuse tomorrow? Also, how do you know what tomorrow will bring? Perhaps something will happen that prevents you from doing the task then, too. A better question to ask yourself is: Why wait until tomorrow if you can get it done now.

Procrastination is a huge problem in our society, and it leads to a lot of anxiety. This anxiety, in turn, leads to a lack of self-confidence. Procrastination is basically a form of being unprepared. Let's say you have a project due on Friday, and it is now Monday. If you begin working on it now, and do a little bit each day, you will have more confidence in completing the project and doing it well, than you would if you started on Thursday. Imagine how much more thorough you can be by starting projects a little bit earlier. The following are a few easy action steps you can take to help overcome procrastination.

- Do not take on more than you can handle. Keep the number of decisions you have to make to a minimum. The more you have to decide on, the more likely you are to procrastinate.

- Begin focusing on the benefits of completing something, rather than the task. For example, if you are working on a project for work, imagine how good it will feel when it's done. Also, think about the rewards that might come if you perform the task well, like a promotion or raise. This focus on the benefits will give you more motivation to get started.

- Prepare yourself for a task by becoming educated on it. Be aware of your limitations before even picking up a new project and do what you can to obtain the necessary knowledge before moving forward. Once again, knowledge will lead to confidence, and confidence makes you active in a pursuit.

- Turn distractions into rewards. If you cannot get your work done because you are always binge-watching shows, then force yourself to turn them into rewards after a hard day's work. For example, set a timer for three hours and use that time to focus on your projects. After the three hours, pat yourself on the back and watch an episode of the show you like. Remember that you have to stay disciplined.

- Set up a daily schedule system for yourself. For example, the first two hours in the morning are designated for the most important tasks, then a break, followed by two hours of the less important tasks, then another break, and finally, dedicating the last part of the day towards the least important tasks. Once you set up a schedule, stick to it to the best of your ability.
- Avoid getting stuck on a project. Give yourself a certain amount of time on a specific task, and if you cannot make progress, move onto something else and revisit it later. There is no sense in wasting time being nonproductive on something.

Follow these steps religiously and watch procrastination be an afterthought in your life.

Build Confidence At Work

Our jobs are a major part of our lives, and it is important to have self-confidence in this environment. We went over building self-confidence in the general sense earlier in this chapter, and now we will focus on more specific areas in our lives. Many of the action steps and techniques are still the same, while some will be more geared towards work.

- Cut out the negative self-talk. Do not beat yourself up at work. It will do nothing for you. Speaking kindly and encouragingly to yourself and you will learn from whatever mistakes you made more easily.

- Boost your knowledge any way you can, and it is a surefire way to achieve confidence. Stay up on the latest research, services, and products within your company and industry as a whole. Imagine being able to bring an idea to your workplace simply because you read up on it. This will make you feel very good about yourself. Always try to stay ahead of the curve.

- Use opportunities to teach others who know less about a subject than you do. Being able to teach others effectively will boot your own knowledge and confidence.

- Practice what you know incessantly, and always look for ways to improve. Identify and correct mistakes along the way.

- Do not speak poorly about others. This already shows a lack of confidence in yourself. When you compliment and speak highly of other people, you acknowledge their strengths and make them feel good about themselves. In turn, you feel good about yourself, too. This also helps to build a nontoxic work environment.

- Pick up new skills to enhance proficiency at your job.

- Ask questions when you do not know something. You may think that you will feel stupid if you ask a question. However, asking and then doing it right, is a bigger boost to confidence than not asking and screwing things up.

- Eliminate negative language, even if it's not geared at anybody. Negative language can affect our psyche on the deepest levels, effectively lowering our confidence levels without us even realizing it.

- Focus on all of the success you have had at work, rather than the failures.

Chapter 4: Getting Rid of Social Anxiety

Social anxiety encompasses many areas of our lives, such as personal relationships, engaging in activities, hanging out in large groups, or giving public speeches. In order to engage in any of these areas, we must overcome our social anxiety, which is essentially having a lack of confidence in social settings. Depending on the individual, social anxiety will either impact them no matter what setting they're, while for others, it will be more selective. For example, a person may be very talkative and confident among his friends but will be terrified when speaking or performing on stage.

This can be the other way around, too. Legendary late-night host, Johnny Carson, was magnanimous on stage but known to be quiet, reserved, and even shy in small groups. We will go over some basic techniques to improve your social anxiety. These will be effective in just about any setting you are in. These techniques are involved with cognitive behavioral therapy, which is a psychologically-based approach to dealing with anxiety, that is drugfree.

- Think about what you're avoiding. As always, the first step in solving a problem is by identifying what it is. What specific social settings are you avoiding. For instance, some people have stated things like using a public restroom, ordering food at a restaurant, becoming scared in a large group, or speaking up at a meeting. Determine what settings cause your social anxiety. Write these down somewhere so you can keep track.

- Now, take your list that you made and develop some type of rating system. This is used to determine the level of anxiety you might experience in each situation to determine what makes it worse. If you feel the most anxious while giving a public speech, then you can rate that as a 10, and then move down from there. So if being around friends gives you none or very little anxiety, that can be a 0 or 1 rating. These ratings are based mainly on predictions. Basically, we are predicting how we would react in certain social settings.

- The next step is to test your predictions. Go out and put yourself in specific situations that may or may not give you the level of anxiety you predicted. For instance, you may have thought you would be at a level of 9 when meeting someone new at a party, but once you did, it was actually around a 4 rating. You may surprise yourself at how well you can actually cope with your anxiety.

- Identify safety behaviors that you use and work to eliminate them. These are superstitious behaviors that people engage in to make them feel safer. I am not talking about carrying a rabbit's foot. Safety behaviors are things like pre-medicating before a social event, avoiding eye contact, rehearsing what you're going to say, or walking with stiff shoulders. The main problem with these types of behaviors is that you will believe they are the only way to get through an anxiety-casing situation. The more you give up these behaviors, the better your experience will be. Imagine how much better a conversation will be when it's natural, rather than scripted.

- Challenge your anxious thoughts. Instead of thinking about how bad things will go, start thinking about how they will go well. If you are worried about looking foolish, ask yourself why that is, and when have you actually looked foolish in the past? Is it real or made up in your head.

- Practice doing what makes you anxious. The classic example here is giving a speech in front of a mirror or recording yourself while you speak alone in your living room. Remind yourself that people don't usually know what your internal feelings are unless you make it obvious to them. This means that no one may have noticed your anxiety in the past. Eventually, test out what you've practiced in the real world. In the case of a speech, after practicing alone for a while, you can perform it in front of some friends.

- Practice self-reward, rather than post-mortem. Post-mortem means that a person analyzes and criticizes every little thing that they've done during a social encounter. If they were standing awkwardly, they become focused on that. Instead, reward yourself for facing the anxiety-causing situation.

Remember to always rinse and repeat with all of these techniques. They must be done regularly until you develop a pattern. You will never be fully confident in every situation. The world will throw things at you that will make you take a few steps back and throw you off your game. That is okay. The key to these exercises is to build up a certain level of self-confidence so that you will be ready to engage and deal with whatever life throws at you. You will develop true strength and knowledge to overcome, no matter how unfamiliar a situation is.

PART II

Chapter 1: Self-Esteem and Valuing Yourself

Imagine waking up in the morning and being full of life. You are energetic as you get out of bed and are ready to attack the day because nothing can stop you. Any type of challenge that comes your way, you are prepared to face it head-on and overcome it. You take pride in your work and relationships because you understand their worth. You also understand the value that you bring to the day, so you carry yourself with strength and dignity.

On the other hand, picture yourself waking up in a crummy mood. You are not looking forward to the day ahead, and no matter what good things may come, they are quickly tossed aside, and your mind wanders towards the negative side. You suffer from anxiety throughout the day, and you avoid any challenging situation you can because you lack faith in yourself.

These two mindsets are entirely different from one another, but they are related to the same thing: Your self-esteem. Self-esteem is the amount of respect that you place on yourself. It is how much you value your skills and ability to handle life and all its circumstances. Those who place a high value on themselves have a high level of self-esteem. Those who set a low value on themselves suffer from low self-esteem.

Your self-esteem is also your self-worth, and you mustn't put a low price tag on your abilities.

Having high self-esteem does not mean you ignore your flaws. It means that you love yourself despite all of them. You recognize your weaknesses, and therefore, are more likely to fix them. In the end, you love yourself because of your own self-beliefs.

As we grow up, we are constantly surrounded by things that affect our psyche. Our ego is the part of our mind that has a direct relationship with the outside world. When we experience an event or interact with a specific individual, it will determine how we feel at that exact moment. If the situation is upsetting, then it can bring out a range of different emotions in us. For those who are dealing with low self-esteem, they will easily be triggered by an outside event. For example, if someone calls us a negative name, it might make us feel sad or angry. This one incident could ruin our whole day in an instant. If we are experiencing negativity over a long period of time, then these thoughts will slowly enter into our subconscious and unconscious mind, where they stay forever, unless we purposefully remove them.

If you have a healthy level of self-esteem, then these situations will roll off your back. Negative people or situations will not change the feelings you have towards yourself because you will be in complete control of your emotions. I am not suggesting that being insulted will not be hurtful for this type of individual, but they will understand how to manage it and not let it affect them negatively. They don't define themselves by other people's opinions.

I can talk all day about the extreme benefits of self-esteem, as there are many. The focus of this book, though, is how to develop and build your self-esteem, even if you have been suffering from low levels of it your whole life. I am working off the assumption that you are in the camp of low self-esteem. Therefore, you already know how it feels, because you are personally living it.

How Low Self-Esteem Is Developed

The first step in dealing with low self-esteem is recognizing that you have it. Now that we have established that, it is important to determine why you have low self-esteem.

The Different Types of Parents

One of the major contributing factors to our self-esteem is our parents and how they raised us. Our mother and father are generally the first people we become close to. How they interact with us will initially determine how we value ourselves. Even if a parent is loving, there are still specific tendencies that can be counterproductive to use raising our self-worth.

While parents often push their children to succeed, some can become overbearing to the point where they use ridicule, harsh criticisms, and even abuse to ensure their children stay on the straight path. While some parents do not have malicious intent when they become disapproving authority figures, others will purposefully look down on their kids and make them feel inferior. Children who grow up under these conditions grow into adults who are never comfortable in their own skin.

On the opposite end of the overbearing caregiver is the uninvolved caregiver who does not care one bit. They ignore their children as if they are not necessary. In fairness, this can often be done unintentionally. For example, the parents work so much and become excessively focused on their jobs. They are obsessed with making a living and ignore the people closest to them, including their children. When children get ignored by the influential adults in their lives, they become confused about their place in the world. They feel forgotten and unimportant, and therefore, they believe their existence to be bothersome to people.

Another parental issue that affects children is the parents or caregivers who are in constant conflict. When these adults fight and throw hurtful language at one another, especially in front of children, they absorb these negative emotions. These children can feel like they contributed to the fighting in some way. Growing into adulthood, these same children will feel like they are the cause of so many different conflicts, simply because they were nearby.

Bullying

Bullying has been an issue for children and adults alike for generations.

The powerful always seem to push around the weak. With children, this power is usually in the form of physical dominance. The bigger and stronger child picks on the smaller and weaker one. Of course, the bullying can be mental or psychological, too, if the child can pull it off.

Bullying can also become a significant contributor to low self-esteem. A child who is constantly bullied in any way will develop a poor self-image about themselves. Unfortunately, bullying will never go away. What matters in these situations is the support that children receive from their parents. The way the adults in a child's life handle the aftermath of bullying will play a major role in their mindset development.

Many children do not have a comforting environment to come home to, which is detrimental to their psyche. After experiencing abuse outside the come, they walk through their front door and experience even more of it. This makes a child feel worthless and abandoned. They become lost further into the abyss and think they do not belong anywhere. Having unsupportive parents will magnify the effects of bullying.

Furthermore, some parents were over-supportive. These are the ones who coddled their children and gave them no coping skills to deal with the outside world. As a result, they will be ill-prepared to deal with the cruel world that exists out there, which is not going away anytime soon. When children become adults and enter the real world, they will face some harsh criticisms that will challenge their beliefs about who they are. If they were always buttered up as children, they would not understand how to face rejection, insults, or people being mean to them.

No parent wants their children to feel bad, but they cannot be shielded from disappointment their whole lives. Once they do face this disappointment in the real world, they will fall apart because they have no actual self-worth. All of their value is tied to the compliments that other people give them.

I know I have been singling out parents here, and that's because they are the adults a child spends the most amount of time with. However, other adults, like extended family members, teachers, coaches, or counselors, can also do their part in providing a supportive atmosphere for the children in their lives.

Trauma

Trauma can be physical, emotional, or sexual, and no matter what kind you were a victim of, it will devastate your self-esteem, especially as a child. With trauma, you are being forced into a position against your will, which makes you feel like you've lost power and control of your situation.

Situations like this will make you feel worthless. You will even blame yourself for causing the trauma or abuse. This is a method many people use to gain control back into their lives. They believe that by taking the blame, they will be able to manage the situation the next time it comes around

Children do not have control over who is in their lives. This means they are often stuck in abusive situations and have no way of getting out of it. If they are lucky, someone will recognize it, and they will help them get out.

A child who goes through trauma will grow into an adult who is unsure of themselves in many ways. They will never feel like they are good enough, will always feel like they are to blame for specific situations, and will have a distrust for humanity in general.

I know I have spoken about a lack of trust throughout this book. A significant part of having self-esteem is being able to put your faith into the unknown. When you lack trust, this faith does not exist, and therefore, you will always be paranoid and never fully confident in any situation.

Now, think back on your life and determine the traumatic events you may have gone through. How did these affect your psyche at that moment? How you felt on the inside when these various circumstances occurred will help you understand if they contributed to a lack of self-esteem.

We went over these issues simply to help you recognize the underlying causes of the value you place on yourself. There is nothing we can do about these situations now, but we can learn from them and work on ways to overcome our mental blocks to positive self-esteem.

The Science of Self-Esteem

There has been a lot of research done on the genetic components of low self-esteem. While people can be born with certain levels of chemicals that influence their emotions and brain activity, there is no conclusive evidence that people are born with high or low self-esteem. Even twins who grew up in different environments were found to have different qualities related to their self-worth, even though various other personality traits were similar. As of now, environmental factors seem to play a much more significant role.

Of course, this does not mean that there is no scientific component to all of this. As we go through various life stages, our brain development occurs based on life experiences. The actions we take and the thoughts we create make numerous neural pathways in our brain and nervous system, which determine our future behavior. For example, if we continuously have negative feelings, our mind becomes wired in a certain way to produce these same thoughts in the future. As a result, you habitually think negatively in every situation you come across.

Now that we have established what low self-esteem is, our goal in the next chapter is to help you rewire your brain, so you can start living with high self-esteem.

Chapter 2: How You Can Matter to Yourself

"Confront the dark parts of yourself, and work to banish them with illumination and forgiveness. Your willingness to wrestle with your demons will cause your angels to sing."

-August Summer

Now that we know what self-esteem is, it is hard to deny the role it plays in our lives. Any type of pursuit, whether personal, professional, relationships, or health, will require you to place a high value on yourself; otherwise, you will never progress forward as you should. At this moment, I want you to recognize the past mistakes that brought you to where you are now, but also forgive yourself for them because you can do nothing to change the past. You can learn from it, though, and build a new future where you actually value yourself and the gifts you bring to the world.

In the previous chapter, we discussed the numerous causes of low self-esteem, many of which stem from our childhood. Since our mindset took a long time to develop, it will take extreme effort with several actionable steps to change and overcome this thought-process. We will now discuss some specific steps and practices over the next few chapters you can engage in to improve your mindset and build-up your self-esteem.

We will approach this subject from many different aspects, so they can be combined to improve how you habitually think about yourself. Think of your mind as a structure that is built to think a specific way. Now imagine having to rebuild many different parts of that structure to change your thoughts. This is what we will be doing with all of the action steps we will go over.

How to Build Self-Awareness

Self-awareness means having the ability to understand the way you think, feel, and behave. This is a necessary quality to have if you want to fix your self-esteem. It is the best way to recognize if your actions correlate with low self-esteem. Once you become self-aware, you will know yourself much better. The following are some significant strategies you can employ right away.

Recognize What Bothers You About Other People

What bothers us most about other people are often the same qualities that we possess. For example, if someone is naturally aggressive, we may dislike it; however, it is a trait that we have, as well. We all have aspects of our personality that are unflattering, and since we don't want to admit them, we will ignore them fully. Ignorance is not bliss in the long-run, and if we do not pay attention to our negative qualities, they will rear their ugly heads at the most inopportune time. The next time a person is bothering you, stop and ask yourself if they are displaying something that is a reflection of you. Do you recognize their personality when you look in the mirror?

Meditate on Your Mind

Mindful meditation is a great way to learn about your thoughts and how they work. One of the main reasons we lack self-awareness is because we are thinking so much that our thoughts completely take over. Proper meditation allows us to separate ourselves from these thoughts and recognize that they do not fully encompass who we are. Through mindful meditation practices, you have the ability to observe your thoughts without becoming attached to them. Therefore, it is easier to see which ones deserve our attention and which ones do not. The following are some simple steps to get you started on this practice.

- Get comfortable by finding a quiet place that is as free from distractions as possible.
- Sit up with your back straight and chest out. It does not matter if you are in a chair or sitting cross-legged on the floor. You may even lie down flat on the floor.
- Take in some deep breaths through your nose and then out slowly through your mouth or nose. You should be able to feel the breaths down into your abdomen. This will help you relax.
- Pay attention to the sounds of your breaths and their rhythmic patterns. When you inhale, imagine breathing in joy and peace. When you breathe out, imagine getting rid of the toxicity in your mind.

- When you notice your thoughts wandering away from your breaths, immediately focus them back to the center. Take in your immediate surroundings and be in your present state. Do not think of the past or worry about the future.
- Make this practice a habit and do it routinely. Some of the best practitioners of mindful meditation have been doing it for years, and are still learning better ways to improve. These are all great steps to get you started and reorganize your mind.

As a side note, meditation is not only useful for self-awareness. It can help with stress and anxiety, communication, better sleep, improved focus on your goals, and overall mental health. All of this will lead back to higher self-esteem. Start off with five minutes and then build yourself up to 20-30. You will be amazed at how much clarity you will have about yourself.

Draw a Timeline of Your Life

Sit down with a notepad and try to remember as much as you can from the time of birth to where you are now. Pay special attention to significant moments that had a big impact on your life and circumstances, whether positive or negative. This practice will allow you to see certain moments of your life in context, which will give you a better idea of who you are. You will realize a lot about yourself and gain much self-awareness.

Identify Your Emotional Kryptonite

Think about the emotions that you absolutely hate having and try to avoid. For example, some individuals hate feeling sad so much that they drown this emotion with alcohol. The problem is, negative emotions are a gateway into our souls. They are trying to tell us something in a discrete way. If we pay attention to them as they are happening, we will learn a lot about our situation. If you are sad often, pay attention to why so you can finally address it.

Travel and Get Out a Little Bit

We often become stuck in our own little box and forget that there is a big world out there. Micro-travel, which means traveling to new destinations that are local to us, is a great way to get you out of your comfort zone and try out a new routine. Take frequent short trips if you can, and even travel abroad if this is feasible. This will help you gain a lot of awareness for the world around you, as well as teach you a lot about yourself. Travel to new destinations, even nearby, will significantly raise our self-awareness.

Pick Up a New Skill

Just like with travel, learning a new skill will force us to think and act in new ways, thereby forcing us to increase our self-awareness. We all develop certain routines as we grow older, and it causes us to go into a comfort zone. The main problem here is that it creates a strong, narrow-mindedness. Being willing to start something as a beginner will cultivate a level of flexibility in our minds and thoughts. The new skill does not have to be related to your career. It can also be hobbies like playing the piano, sculpting, or dancing.

Clarify Your True Values

How often do you sit down and assess what your true values are? If you are like most people, probably very seldomly. We often get so caught up in daily life that we have very little time for self-reflection, especially on the important things in life. As a result, we end up chasing false goals and not living the type of life we want to. People become so worried about moving up the career ladder and buying the latest fancy car, that they forget what actually makes them happy. In your case, you may have followed a safe career path rather than focus on what your true calling was.

A great technique you can perform is to set aside some time on a weekly or monthly basis and think about your life and circumstances. Ask yourself why you think you are here and what your purpose in life is? Also, imagine what a fulfilling life would look like for you. Spend about 30 minutes every time you do this. A major part of self-awareness is recognizing what really matters to you. This practice will be a great way to come to this understanding.

We tend to get lost in the monotony of life. So, it is important to practice these self-awareness techniques on a regular basis. Taking notice of your thoughts, behaviors, and actions in real-time is a special skill to have. It will go a long way in helping you build your self-esteem.

Chapter 3: Creating a Stronger Self

Going along the path of improved self-esteem, I will now discuss various strategies to strengthen your psyche. High self-esteem requires a strong mindset.

Managing Your Ego

I spoke briefly in chapter one about the ego. Our ego is basically our mind's direct connection to the outside world. What our environment gives, our ego responds. This means that whatever activities are going on around will make you feel a certain way, and this is directly the result based on how our ego responds. For example, if someone outshines us in some way, our ego will respond by making us feel inferior.

People who are not careful will have this aspect of the mind completely control them. As a result, the values they place on themselves are based on what the world thinks of them, rather than what they think of themselves. Every one of us has an ego to a certain degree, but the key is to not let it control us. We must learn to manage it properly so that our self-worth comes from within, rather than from what we can't control. The following are specific steps you can take to begin managing your ego so that it doesn't control you.

Don't Take Things Personally

Taking things too personally or literally can make you overthink and cause your mind to become infected. It's important to be at peace with yourself and realize that people do not always mean what they say. They are often angry or suffering from some other negative emotion. Even if they do mean it, people who treat others poorly have a problem within themselves, and not necessarily other people. In a moment where you are facing harsh words or actions, imagine your spot being replaced by someone else and watching the same people act in the same manner because, in most cases, they would. A big part of self-esteem is not caring what others think. This is a major step in that direction.

Accepts All of Your Mistakes

Accepting your mistakes, no matter how big or small is a positive way to work on your ego problems. Everyone makes mistakes, so there is no use in hiding them. Once you admit them, apologize, and move on, they no longer have control over you as you've released them from your psyche. Genuinely apologizing to someone is a great way to put your ego in check and grow as a person.

Stop Being Self-Conscious

Our ego prevents us from looking silly or goofy. We are so afraid of what others are thinking that we never let out guard down. This is a real definition of living in fear. If you have been acting this way for a while, then it's time to stop putting up a shield, and just let your silly self come out. You will actually be happier in the long run because showcasing your true self will attract your real friends. To stop being so self-conscious, try using the following steps.

- Shrug away your negative thoughts. This does not mean you should ignore them. Acknowledge that they are there, but then do not agree with them in any way.

- Don't put other people on pedestals. We have a tendency to do this, especially to those who we admire. Realize that they are regular people and not someone to bow down to.

- Think of a moment where you were self-conscious, and then imagine replacing yourself with someone you cared about in the position. If they felt the same way you did, then what would you tell them. Now, tell that same thing to yourself. We are often bigger critics of ourselves than we are other people.

- Accept yourself, with your faults and all. Remember that nobody is perfect, and if you want to gain a high level of self-esteem, then you must learn to love yourself, including your flaws.

- People are not paying as much attention to you as you may think. Part of our ego tells us that people are watching us and critiquing our every move. Understand that people are in their own world much of the time, and too busy in their personal self-doubts to pay attention to anyone else. Believe it or not, you are not the focus of attention all the time.

- Go do the thing that makes you self-conscious or nervous. Face it head-on, and you will realize it's not as bad as you may think. Do not let your awkwardness keep you on the sidelines. Jump in with both feet and dare to look foolish. If you hate dancing in front of people, join a dance class and do it several times a week. If you suck at basketball, go to the part and shoot hoops in front of people.

Realize That Your Ego Will Never Go Away

Controlling and managing your ego will have to become a routine in your life. It will never fully go away and will rear its ugly head at the most inopportune times if you let your guard down. Always be on high alert of your ego trying to take over, and you will continue to overcome it.

You Are Not the Best

I am not trying to be insulting here, but knowing that you are not going to be the best in every situation means that you understand your limitations. Everyone has limitations, so there is no sense in feeling bad over them. Accept that you are not perfect, but recognize that it does mean you cannot accomplish your goals. You may just need to work harder and focus more on certain areas.

Imagine Your Ego as Another Person

This step may seem ridiculous, but imagine your ego as another person. It is best to picture someone that you may listen, but never actually take advice from, like a whining child. Now, once you imagine your ego in this manner, allow it to speak and say what it needs, acknowledge it with a "thank you," and then move on. When you can actually picture your ego in this way, it will do a lot in stopping you from making significant mistakes.

Stop Bragging

There is no need to brag about your accomplishments. If they are great enough, other people will do the talking for you. The less you talk about yourself, the more humble you become, and humility is a major aspect of self-esteem. You never feel the need to talk yourself up.

Be Grateful for the Little Things

Gratitude is great for improving your attitude. When you start being grateful for the little things, you do not worry so much about the big things. Also, remember that some people cannot have what you have, no matter how hard they try. With the same token, some people will be in a different position than you, that you are unable to reach. That is okay. Just focus on yourself and what you have.

Learn to Compliment Others

People with large egos have a hard time admitting when others have done a great job. They feel it will take the spotlight off of them. Practicing paying even the smallest compliments to other people can help you take the attention off of your ego problems.

On top of these practices, we have gone over, a few other ways to get rid of your ego include:

- Embrace a beginner's attitude. Try something new regularly that forces you to challenge yourself. This will help you realize that you are not perfect at everything.
- Concentrate on the effort you put in, and not the results. You will be forced to see how much you put into an activity, and determine if you did too much, or not enough.
- Never stop learning, even if it's not something you will ever use. It keeps you humble.
- Validate yourself once in a while.
- Never expect rewards or recognition. Do what is right, simply because it is the right thing to do.
- Do not try to control everything.

Forgiving People

Since so much of our self-esteem is tied up in what the people of our past did or did not do for us, it is important to forgive those who may have harmed us. We often hold onto grudges, and this prevents us from moving forward. Part of having self-esteem is no longer allowing others to control us. If the actions of people in the past still impact the opinion we have of ourselves, then we are still under there control. The main idea of forgiveness is that you have the ability to move on without having to carry a heavy burden any longer. Here is what forgiveness does not mean:

- Condoning harmful behavior.
- Accepting someone back into your life.
- Forgetting the incident or incidents that harmed you.
- Having to talk to the person again in any way.
- You are helping the other person. Of course, this may be a secondary benefit, which is fine.

By forgiving someone, you are accepting the reality that they did something terrible to you, but it no longer has to define you. Forgiveness is 100 percent for your own benefit.

The first step in forgiveness is the willingness to actually forgive someone. Just imagine that the anger you have for someone is a bag of rocks that you have been carrying on your back. After many years, this becomes very exhausting, both physically and mentally. Now, imagine that forgiveness means dropping that bag of rocks forever. You will feel much better when you put down the bag, and you will feel much better once you forgive. When you are ready, then utilize the following steps to help you get past, well, your past.

- Think about the particular incidents that angered you. Accept that they happened and what your feelings were when they did. In order to forgive, you must acknowledge what happened. You cannot just ignore it. This is why forgetting is not part of the process. For example, the incident could have been that your parents were absent and did not pay any attention to you.

- Acknowledge the growth in yourself that happened after the incident occurred. What did it make you learn about yourself and the world? For example, if your parents were absent for much of your life, perhaps it taught you how to be independent and survive on your own. That is a pretty big deal.

- Now think about the other person. The one that actually caused the incident. Realize that they were working from a limited frame of mind and did not have the benefit of hindsight. When they harmed you in some way, they were probably trying to have one of their needs met. Think about what that need may have been, and if it changes your perspective on them. In reference to your parents, maybe they were absent and did not pay attention to you because they were worried about always having food on the table and a roof over your head. This caused them to work incessantly, and when they were home, they were too tired to give you the right amount of attention. It's possible that they hated being absent just as much as you did.

- Finally, say the words, "I forgive you." It is up to you whether you want to tell the person or not. In any event, tell yourself.

Forgiveness will help you put closure on your past so that you can focus on moving forward. This is an important step forward to gaining self-esteem. You will no longer be bound by what happened to you in the past; therefore, you will be free.

Overcoming Trauma

Since trauma plays a major role in a person's self-image, it is important to identify the negative thoughts that will lead to low self-esteem. Once you catch these thoughts, then you can combat them head-on. You may never forget about the trauma, but just like the hurt you received from people of your past, you can keep it from controlling you. The following are a few simple steps you can take to help you improve your negative self-image related to trauma. These practices have been used widely with people suffering from Post Traumatic Stress Disorder.

- Identify your negative thoughts. Once negative thoughts become part of your routine, they can easily slip by without getting caught. Self-monitoring can be a great way of increasing awareness of your thoughts and how they are affecting your mood and behavior. You must do this consciously. You may also sit down at the end of each day and run down what you did. Think about all of the negative thoughts you had, what caused them, and how you reacted. This can also make you more aware of them in the future. We often have specific triggers that affect our mood.

- Once you learn to identify negative thoughts, slow them down. The more you think about negative thoughts, the more intense they become. Therefore, once you identify them, distract yourself by thinking of something else. This is not about avoidance, but taking a step back and reducing the intensity of these thoughts. Often times, we cannot deal with negativity because it becomes so overwhelming. Once we remove ourselves from the situation a little bit, then we can manage things more appropriately.

- After reducing the intensity of your thoughts, it is now time to challenge them. Many times, we accept our thoughts at face value without actually questioning them. As a result, we do not actually know why we are thinking negatively during a certain situation. We just know that we always have. Challenge your thoughts by asking some of the following questions:

    - What evidence is there for having these thoughts?
    - What evidence is there that are against these thoughts?
    - Are there moments when these thoughts have not been true?
    - Do I only have these thoughts when I am sad, angry, or depressed, or do I have them when I am feeling okay, as well?
    - What advice would I give someone else who is also having these thoughts?

- Is there any type of alternate explanation?

- Counter your negative thoughts further by using positive self-supportive statements. For example, you can tell yourself all of your recent accomplishments, the good qualities you do possess, or positive things you are looking forward to in the future, like starting a new job or taking a vacation. Basically, counter negative thoughts with positive ones. It is beneficial to write some of these down so you can refer to them in the future. When you are drowning in negativity, it can be difficult to come up with positive statements about yourself.

- As a side note, you do not have to use positive self-supportive statements exclusively when you are upset. You can tell them to yourself any time to build up your positivity.

Chapter 4: Changing Our Minds

For the final chapter in this section, we can start focusing on shifting the mindest fully towards high self-esteem. Once this occurs, we must continue to follow the strategies I have gone over to never lose your self-esteem. If you let your guard down, it will happen.

How To Ignore Things

Our self-esteem continues to remain low throughout our lives because we always let things bother us. Many of these things are beyond our control, so we should not pay them any mind. The reason people achieve their lifelong goals is that they don't let their surroundings affect their minds. The following are some ways to ignore what bothers you, so you can keep moving forward while loving yourself.

Stop Comparing Yourself To Others

The bottom line is, you are not someone else, and they are not you. Just because someone else looks great in a dress or suit, does not mean you have to, as well. Also, understand that other people will not look as good as you in certain outfits. Some people will look great all dressed up, while others pull off the casual look better.

If you are not comfortable, then you will never feel right in any situation. Therefore, do not force yourself into something, simply because other people are doing it. Understand yourself through self-awareness and focus on the things that make you feel good. You can't compare yourself to others, and they can't compare themselves to you. Work on impressing the person in the mirror and no one else.

Ignore Societal Pressure

Have you ever done something because someone you don't like or even know might become impressed, even though they don't actually care about you? If this statement sounds ridiculous, imagine actually living. Oh, wait! Many people are already. This is because they are under some sort of societal pressure to live a certain way, even though most people in society don't matter to them in the long run. To stop allowing this to happen, ask yourself the following questions.

- Who will be responsible after I kill my dreams to produce a fake image, society, or me?
- Are the people around me genuinely concerned about my happiness? If not, then why do I care so much?
- Will the people pressuring me even matter five years from now?
- Am I alone in feeling this societal pressure?

After answering all of these questions, you will realize that your situation is not unique. Many people are pressured by society and trying to hold up a fake image. This means they are not happy because they are not willing to share their true selves. Ultimately, you will be living your own existence, whether you choose it or someone else does.

Start Living In The Present Moment

So many people live in the past, and therefore, their old mistakes still have an impact on their present state of mind. It's time to get over your past. The following are some tips to help you do so.

- Create some physical distance between yourself and the person or situation that is reminding you of your past. This could mean cutting off some close people or physically moving somewhere else.
- Stay busy working and improving yourself, that you have no time to worry about what happened in the past.
- Treat yourself like you would a best friend. We tend to be gentler with others than ourselves.
- Don't shut out negative emotions. Let them flow through you so you can overcome them.
- Don't expect an apology from other people. Even if you were wronged by them, they might not think so. Therefore, move on and accept that they haven't come to terms with anything, but you have.
- Give yourself permission to talk about your pain, even if it's just to yourself. In any event, let it out. Let the past pain escape out of you.

Leverage Your Purpose

This will give your life more meaning. First, leverage your purpose to serve others. Help someone else realize their dreams through your own unique talents. There are many unique ways to do this, including teaching, coaching, and mentoring. Do this on a volunteer basis. Whatever gives purpose to your life, share it with someone else.

Try out these different practices and feel yourself start ignoring all of the noise around you. It is distracting, and you must be able to filter it.

The Mindset Shift

We have gone over many different aspects of the mind and how to change certain thought-processes. What happens with these techniques is a total mindset shift. Instead of your mind being wired to think negatively about everything, including yourself, you will now habitually think in a positive way and understand the values you bring to the world, which are a lot. The goal of all of the previous practices and strategies is to rewire your neural pathways to help change your mindset.

Your mindset was developed over a long period of time, which means the neural pathways you have are build up pretty strong. For this reason, they must be worked on regularly to help break them down and build new ones up. So, do not treat these techniques as a one-and-done cure. They must become a regular part of your lifestyle. Once they are, then you will be amazed at the results you have. When your self-esteem is high, you will:

- Have no problem being yourself.
- Be able to disagree without attacking someone.
- Not be swayed so easily by the opinions of others.
- Be able to articulate your views and be able to defend them appropriately when challenged.
- No longer fear uncertainty.
- Be much more resilient and tough.
- Never need approval from anyone to live your life as you choose.
- Value yourself and have high self-worth, despite what others may think of you.
- Not act like you know everything.
- Be okay with not being perfect.
- Never again let your past define who you are.

Once you go from low to high self-esteem, you will feel like a completely different person. You will still acknowledge your past pain, but it will not control you.

Now That Your Self-Esteem is High

After going through all of the practices, thoughts, and feelings inside of you will be different because you will have effectively restructured your mind. The plan now is to keep revisiting these techniques, so you never fall back into the abyss ever again. Now that your self-esteem is high, you will sense the following beliefs flowing through you.

- No matter what you've done, you are worthy of love. You understand your past mistakes, but will not degrade yourself over them.
- You are not defined by your "stuff." You will enjoy what you have, but your happiness will not be dependent on it.
- You will allow yourself to feel all of your emotions, and not be ashamed of them.
- You won't care if you miss out on things. You will feel okay about staying alone because your company is good enough.
- You will not be worried about what happens to you, because you will be able to respond appropriately, There will be challenges, but the end result will be in your favor.
- You will be doing what you love. You will look forward to every day.
- You will understand that people are judging you based on something within themselves.
- You will never think the world revolves around you. There is a higher power out there greater than anything that exists on Earth. This does not have to be a diety, but it certainly can be for you.
- You will find things to be grateful for every day. Because you are looking, you will find them.
-

PART III

Chapter 1- What is Self Compassion

What is the self-compassion? Have you thought about it or experienced it from someone?

The truth is, having compassion for yourself is not different from having compassion for other people or animals. Having self-compassion is being kind to yourself and understanding to your needs when you face personal failures. Think about how you would talk and console a friend who's going through a rough time- what would you say to them? Would you be harsh to them? Would you say things that bring them down even more?

The answers to those questions are of course a big NO. You would do what all good friends do- bring them up when they feel down, hug them and tell them everything is going to be ok, telling them that you'll be there for them to talk to or if they need help. Self-compassion is acting this same way towards yourself when you go through a rough patch. You notice the suffering and you empathize with yourself by comforting yourself, offering kindness and understanding.

Kristin D. Neff and Katie A. Dahm are two prominent are two names synonymous with the research on self-compassion. In their book, the Handbook of Mindfulness and Self-Regulation, it states that there are three primary components to self-compassion:

1. Self-kindness
2. Common humanity
3. Mindfulness

To understand self compassion, we need to consider what it means to feel compassion on a general level. Here are some views of compassion:

The Buddhist point of view of compassion is given to our own as well as to others suffering.

Goetz, Keltner & Simon- Thomans, 2010: Compassion is the sensitivity to the suffering that is happening, coupled with a deep desire to alleviate that suffering

Neff, 2003a: Self-compassion is compassion directed inwards, referring to ourselves as the object of concern and care when we are faced with an experience of suffering

The Three Elements of Self-Compassion

The key to understanding self-compassion is to understand the difference between this trait and more negative ones. Sometimes when we give ourselves self-compassion, it may be construed as narcissism to a point, which is why it is important to know what is self-compassion and to what degree is it considered self-compassion and when it isn't.

1. *Self-kindness is not Self-Judgement*

Self-compassion is being understanding and warm to ourselves when we fail, or when we suffer or at moments when we feel inadequate. We should not be ignoring these emotions or criticizing yourself. People who have self-compassion understand that being human comes with its own imperfections and failing is part of the human experience. It is inevitable that there will be no failure when we attempt something because failure is part of learning and progress. We will look into how failure is a friend in disguise in the next chapters. Having self-compassion is also being gentle with yourself when faced with painful experiences rather than getting angry at everything and anything that falls short of your goals and ideals.

Things cannot be exactly the way it should be or supposed to be or how we dream it to be. There will be changes and when we accept this with kindness and sympathy and understanding, we experience greater emotional equanimity.

2. *Common humanity and not Isolation*

It is a common human emotion to feel frustrated especially when things do not go the way we envision them to be. When this happens, frustration is usually accompanied by irrational isolation, making us feel and think that we are the only person on earth going through this or making dumb mistakes like this. News flash- all humans suffer, all of us go through different kinds of suffering at varying degrees. Self- compassion involves recognizing that we all suffer and all of us have personal inadequacies. It does not happen to 'Me' or 'I' alone.

3. *Mindfulness is not Over-Identification*

Self-compassion needs us to be balanced with our approach so that our negative emotions are neither exaggerated or suppressed. This balance act comes out from the process of relating our personal experiences with that of the suffering of others. This puts the situation we are going through into a larger perspective.

We need to keep mindful awareness so that we can observe our own negative thoughts and emotions with clarity and openness. Having a mindful approach is non-judgemental and it is a state of mindful reception that enables us to observe our feelings and thoughts without denying them or suppressing them. There is no way that we can ignore our pain and feel compassion at the same time. By having mindfulness, we also prevent over-identification of our thoughts and feelings.

Discovering Self Compassion

You're so dumb! You don't belong here loser! Those jeans make you look like a fat cow! You can't sit with us! It's safe to say we've all heard some kind rude, unwanted comments either directly or indirectly aimed at us. Would you talk like this to a friend? Again, the answer is a big NO.

Believe it or not, it is a lot easier and natural for us to be kind and nice to people than to be mean and rude to them whether it is a stranger or someone we care about in our lives. When someone we care is hurt or is going through a rough time, we console them and say it is ok to fail. We support them when they feel bad about themselves and we comfort them to make them feel better or just to give a shoulder to cry on.

We are all good at being understanding and compassionate and kind to others. How often do we offer this same kindness and compassion to ourselves? Research on self-compassion shows that those who are compassionate are less likely to be anxious, depressed or stressed and more resilient, happy and optimistic. In other words, they have better mental health.

Conclusion

It does make sense that people who have better self-compassion are happier and optimistic about their future. When we continuously criticise ourselves and berate ourselves, we end up feeling incompetent, worthless and insecure. This cycle of negativity continue to self-sabotage us and sometimes, we end up self harming ourselves.

But when our positive inner voice triumphs and plays the role of the supportive friend, we create a sense of safety and we accept ourselves enough to see a better and clear vision. We then work towards making the required changes for us to be healthier and happier. But if we do not do this, we are working ourselves towards a downward spiral or chaos, unhappiness and stress.

In the next chapters, we will look into the benefits of self-compassion, self-esteem, how to get rid of negative self-talk, mastering our emotions as well as practical exercises towards becoming self-compassionate.

Chapter 2- Benefits of Self-Compassion

You've probably heard your parents say time and time again to treat others as you would want them to treat you. Therefore, we are often taught to be empathetic and compassionate to others who are facing difficulties and challenges in their life. However, when faced with our own personnel challenges be it in our everyday lives, work and relationships, we often find ourselves becoming our own worst enemy. Hence we become too critical and judgmental on our own selves and in turn prevent any healing process from taking place.

Therefore, instead of being self-critical to oneself, we need to develop the concept of self-compassion in combating our negative thoughts and self-criticism that keeps us from overcoming our obstacles and challenges.

Self-compassion is defined as being compassionate to our own suffering, inadequacies, weakness and failures. As we know from the previous chapter, Kristin Neff, an associate professor at department of educational psychology in the University of Texas further breaks down self-compassion to 3 key elements which are self-kindness, common humanity and mindfulness.

Self-kindness is about recognizing our flaws and issues as well as being caring to oneself when going through bouts of hardship and challenges. Common humanity on the other hand, puts emphasis that the suffering and anguish we go through is all a natural part of being human and it's a normal part of everyday life. Lastly, mindfulness deals with the individual's ability to take a middle path in addressing their sufferings so as not to neglect or overthinking the situation.

Various research done on the topic of self-compassion indicates that individuals who practice self-compassion have a far greater psychological health than those who lack it. The individuals who practice self-compassion have a more positive life satisfaction, happiness and optimism. Apart from that self-compassion is also connected low levels of anxiety, self-criticism and depression. As such, in a way self-compassion can be used as a tool to develop inner strength when facing challenges in every aspect of our life.

So we know what self-compassion is and sure it helps us lead a better life and have better relationships. What other aspects of self-compassion are there? Here are some major benefits you can reap from being self-compassion. We explore it in terms of work, relationships and in life.

Self-Compassion At Work

Our daily work environment can be a long-lasting love-hate relationship with its own ups and downs that one has to face on a daily basis. As such, we are constantly bombarded with undue stress in meeting deadlines, reports and customer expectations. Many at times, we will face moments that completely overwhelm us and have a negative impact on us. This can be caused by numerous factors such as a negative remark by a colleague, superior or even a customer, failure to reach sales targets or goals, not getting that raise or promotion that you so deserve or even by making an unintentional mistake at the job. Since we all strive to achieve more and be perfect at our jobs, this negative circumstances will have an adverse effect if not dealt properly and swiftly.

Self-compassion can be used at work through the following means to reap various benefits: -

- Conducting a post-mortem to review the shortcomings and failures of a certain project or task and learning from these failures to prevent similar occurrences in the future.
- When facing criticism and rejection from colleagues, superiors and customers, instead of being self-critical and falling into complete despair, we will be able to be calm and focus our energies and thoughts of improving ourselves and not to allow stress to overwhelm ourselves.

- Applying self-compassion at work also helps us in being resilient through difficult scenarios especially is situations that we don't get a certain reward or promotion that we think we deserve.
- Self-compassion enables us to be more creative. When we fail a project or we do not complete a task or when a work event doesn't go as expected, being self-compassionate to ourselves will help us to look back at the series of events and instead of berating ourselves, we look back and see what we could have done better and learn from our mistakes. It makes us becoming more creative the next time around.
- Self-compassion builds trust. It enables you to be transparent and authentic, makes it easier for people to connect with you because you are your true self.
- Showing genuine compassion to yourself also means showing compassion to the people around you. When you show compassion to yourself, you extend this feeling to your co-workers and it makes them feel safe.
- Self compassion allows you to allow yourself and your team implicit permission to do their very best without worry of punishment or repercussions if something doesn't go right.

Self-Compassion In Relationships

In the topic of relationships be it a romantic or non-romantic relationship, we often find ourselves in situations of disagreement from time to time. And these can sometimes lead to moments of stress and unhappiness between oneself and their significant other/parent/sibling/friend. Self-compassion provides various ways much like our situations at work to help us deal with this issues and challenges. Many studies done on this matter point that self-compassion when used have the following positive impact on relationships: -

- Individuals who practice self-compassion know that every individual as well as themselves aren't perfect and are subjected to weaknesses and shortcomings
- They are able relate to their partners much better
- They are more warm and compassionate in understanding a situation
- They are more open to compromising to resolve a situation
- Individuals who are self-compassionate have better empathy. The bring out the best in their partners.
- They are more responsive and aware to the issues that their partner faces
- They are better listeners, they listen to understand and not answer
- People who practice self-compassion own up to their mistakes

Studies also have shown that individuals that lack self-compassion tend to have a negative effect on people around them which may lead to isolation. As such, those people who practice self-compassion have healthier and happier relationships and have a bigger a wide social circle.

Self-Compassion In Life

When encountering difficulties in daily life which can range from a number of issues/aspects such as health to financial issues, we need to act by being compassionate and kind to ourselves. When faced with various issues on a daily basis, self-compassion allows us to look for solutions to take care of oneself instead of berating or being overly critical of one's lack of accomplishments or weaknesses.

With that being said, an individual who practices self-compassion will look into various ways to engage their mind and body into healthy activities that can stimulate them and lets them focus on positive aspects instead of groveling on a negative situation. This can be in a form of an exercise, a hobby, prayer or even a warm bath or a cup of tea to calm themselves down.

Self-compassionate individuals tend to be more: -

- Happier
- Satisfied with life
- Resilient
- Emotionally intelligent
- Have better coping mechanisms
- Optimistic
- Creative
- Less judgemental
- Better goal-getters
- It greatly reduces mental problems

As such, cultivating the habits of self-compassion in every aspect of our life will allow to become the best version of ourselves and allow us to live much happier with the right mindset.

Chapter 3: Myths about Self Compassion

Many people do not have any issues with showing compassion to other people- it is a commendable quality. Compassion is often seen with kindness, tenderness, understanding, sympathy, empathy and of course the impulse to help those in need, whether human or animal.

However, with self-compassion, that is a different story altogether. For plenty of people, having self-compassion often relates to negative qualities such as self-serving, self-pity, self-centered, indulgent and just selfish. We seem to think that if we are not hard on ourselves or punishing ourselves over our failures and flaws, we risk a runaway ego and fall into the traps of false pride.

Take for example, Norman. A young bank executive who is also a new father. Between juggling work and a new baby, he also spends time volunteering as a football coach at a local shelter. He is a committed father and husband, a hard worker and a community role-model. But Norman has gone through several episodes of anxiety attacks simply because he feels overwhelmed, he feels he isn't contributing enough in his team at work and isn't good enough as a husband or father.

People have misgivings about self-compassion and it is only because nobody really knows what it looks like, or even how to practice it so it doesn't become excessive and borderline narcissistic. Self compassion has the element of mindfulness, of wisdom and the recognition to common humanity. Research by Kristin Neff points the myths that people have on self-compassion is the main reason why most of us are in the cycle of criticizing yourself over and over again. Here are the common myths:

#1 Self-Compassion is just a person crying out for self-pity
Let's get this straight- self compassion does not mean you are feeling sorry for

yourself. It is fact an antidote to self-pity. It isn't about whining about our bad luck but instead, self-compassion makes us more open to acknowledging, accepting and experiencing difficult feelings with the help of kindness. Self-compassionate people have a lower tendency of wallowing in self-pity about how bad the circumstances may be and this leads to better mental clarity and mental health.

Filip Raes of the University of Leuven conducted a study on the connection between self-compassion, mental health and ruminative thinking. This study was conducted among the students in his university. Students were first assessed using the Self-Compassion Scale developed by Dr. Kristin Neff. Participants were asked how often they responded to behaviors that corresponded with the main components of self-compassion. These behaviors included "I try to be patient and understanding towards the elements of my personality that I am not fond of"; "When things are going badly for me, I see them as part of life that happens to everyone".

The result of the study showed that students who had better self-compassion parameters were less whiny and broody when things did not go their way. They were also less anxious and less depressed and showed better signs of attentiveness.

#2 Self-compassion is a sign of weakness

Melissa, as a first born child was always seen as the responsible one, a label she has taken on with pride. She sees herself as a pillar of strength to her family. However, since Melissa got married, she has decided to take a step back and pay more attention to her new marriage. While her own family has never imposed on her, Melissa secretly feels as if she is not being a good daughter, and racked with guilt. When her friends suggested that she try not being too hard on herself, her reaction was to immediately tell them off, saying that self-compassion does not make her a good daughter. What Melissa does not know is that this is not a sign of her abandoning her family or a sign of weakness but discovering self-compassion is part of the process of resilience to us. When going through changes in life, self-compassion enables us to survive and thrive.

#3 Self-Compassion can make you a complacent person

Thinking that self-compassion makes you complacent is one of the biggest blocks you can place on yourself. It's so easy for us to criticize ourselves just because we fail to live up to certain standards and we immediately label ourselves as sloths. Do we do this to our kids too?

Amanda's daughter just failed her Biology test and upon finding out, Amanda starts berating her, saying that she is stupid and that she is ashamed of her. This is the exact same thing that Amanda tells herself when she fails to live up to a certain expectation. Rather than motivating her daughter, these comments on her daughter lose faith in herself and prevents her from trying to do better.

What Amanda can do however is practice a more compassionate approach to the situation by giving a hug, telling her daughter that it happens to anyone and what support can she give her daughter. Telling her daughter that she believes in her will help motivate her.

Amanda needs to give honest recognition to the failure as well as empathize with her daughter's unhappiness. This caring response helps us boost out self-confidence and spread emotional support.

While Amanda may not have said those words to her daughter, she still believes deep down that this type of negative feedback may spur her daughter to achieve the necessary goals. But thanks research on human emotions and its responses, showing self-compassion is more effective to boost a better rate of success than self-punishment.

Juliana Breines and Serena Chen of University of California conducted a research to examine the effects of self-compassion and to see how or if it was one of the factors that motivated participants to get involved in positive behaviors and make positive changes. Participants were ask to think back at a time when they felt guilty about such as lying to a partner, cheating in an exam which made them feel bad even till now. They were then randomly assigned to write to themselves from three different perspectives:

1. that of a compassionate and understanding friend
2. write about their own positive qualities
3. write about a hobby they enjoyed doing

Researchers found that participants involved in the self-compassionate perspective were more remorseful for their wrong doing and were more motivated to not repeat the offence.

The research concluded that self-compassion was not about evading personal accountability, rather strengthening it. Acknowledging our failures with kindness rather than judgements enables us to see ourselves clearly beyond the spectacles of self-judgement. Tell ourselves 'I can't believe I messed up. I got so stressed and I overreacted' rather than 'I cannot believe i said that. Why am I so mean?'

#4 Self-Compassions makes us more narcissistic

To many Americans, having high self-esteem means that you are special and beyond average. For some people with high self-esteem, the minute that we receive a less than average score, our self-esteem crashes and plummets. There is no way that everyone to be above average all the time. There are some areas that we can excel because we are naturally good at it but then there are aspects that we either under perform or we are just average. That is why diversity is good. At times when we do perform below average, we see ourselves like failures. The desire to be above average is always going to be there, as we like that feeling of high self-esteem. However this can make us be develop nasty behaviors.

Jean Twenge, a researcher from the San Diego University and Keith Campbell from the University of Georgia have been studying narcissism scores since 1987 among college students. It may not come as a surprise to you to know that among modern-day social media savvy students, narcissism ran high.

It is extremely important to note the difference between self-compassion and self-esteem. While they are both connected to our psychological well-being, the difference is very vivid:

- Self-esteem is evaluating your self-worth positively
- Self-compassion is relating to the changes that happen to us with kindness and acceptance

With self-esteem, we want to feel better than the people around us but with self-compassion, we acknowledge the fact that we have and share certain imperfections. Self-esteem is buoyancy, depending on our latest success or failure. Those with higher levels of self-esteem tend to get upset when they receive neutral feedback. They often start thinking 'Am I just average? I thought i was exceptional'. They are also likelier to listen to any feedback that is related to their personality and blame it on external factors. Self-esteem thrives only when the reviews are good which leads to evasiveness.

Self-compassionate people on the other hand are more emotionally stable despite the degree of praise they receive.

#5 Self-compassion makes us selfish

It is easy to conflate self-compassion with selfishness. Joshua for example spends a large portion of his day caring for his family and at weekends, he supports activities at the local college. He was raised in a family placed importance on service to others. This eventually led him to think that spending time for self-care and being kind and caring to his needs meant he must be neglecting the people around him just for his own needs.

There are plenty of people like Joshua- selfless, good, altruistic and generous to others but horrible to their own selves. When we become too absorbed in self-judgement, we end up giving less because we are preoccupied by thinking about our inadequacies and worthless selves.

Plenty of our emotional needs are met when we are kind and nurturing to ourselves which leaves us in a better position to focus on the people around us. However, caring for the welfare of others often becomes a bigger priority and the idea of treating ourselves badly starts rearing its ugly head. Think about the safety message on an airplane. It is advised to place the oxygen mask over your ownself before assisting others right? This is the same for self compassion.

Kristin Neff conducted a research with Tasha Beretvas of the University of Texas just to prove that being good to ourselves is more helpful when we want to be good to others. The research look at whether people who were self-compassionate were more giving in their relationships. It explored 100 couple who are in romantic relationships for a year or longer. Participants were asked to rate themselves based on the Self-Compassion Scale.

Neff & Beretvas found that partners who were self-compassionate individuals were described as more accepting, caring and supportive compared to self-critical partners who were seen as detached, controlling and aggressive. Self-compassionate partners brought to the table a more secure and satisfied relationship.

A growing research also focuses on therapists and caregivers who were more self-compassionate. Those who were were less likely to feel caregiver burnout and they were more satisfied with their careers, they were more happy, they felt more energized and were more grateful to be able to make a difference.

Conclusion

Self-compassion enables us to feel love, courage, wisdom and generosity in a more sustainable way. It gives us a boundless and directionless mental and emotional state. The power of self-compassion can be enriched through practice and of course through learning, just like so many other good habits.

Being kind to ourselves is not a selfish luxury or a sign of weakness or self-pity. It is a gift to our persons to make us happier and more fulfilled. Thanks to the many research conducted, we now know the myths of self-compassion.

Chapter 4- Dealing with Negativity

Did you ever realize that it is much easier to be happy than it is to be unhappy? Go ahead. Think about it. While you are reading this, just think about the many things that happened before you opening this book and reading. What happened when you woke up? Did you get a kiss from your partner? How did your coffee taste this morning? How is the weather outside like now? All these things that happened to you today, what made you happy and what made you sad?

If you listed ten things today and 7 of them were things that made your happy and three made you unhappy, sad, frustrated or moody, then most likely you were grateful, and you were positive. The thing is, many of us would prefer to be happy and positive rather than be unhappy and negative. And it is that simple to be positive and happy. Also, positive thinking is above and beyond just being happy or displaying a cheerful and upbeat attitude. It also creates and establishes value in your life and relationships, and it also helps you build skills that benefit you longer than your smile can take you. Barbara Fredrickson, a positive psychology researcher from the University of North Carolina, published a landmark paper on the impact of positive thinking on work, health and general wellbeing. Here's a little brief of Barbara's research:

What Can Negative Thinking do to your Brain?

Our brain is programmed to respond to negative emotions by shutting off the world around us and limiting the options we see around us. For example, if you get into a fight with your sister, your emotions and anger might consume to the point where you react adversely- you can't think about anything else. Or for instance your coffee this morning spilled on your shirt, and this creates a domino effect of everything going wrong in your day, and you get so stressed out that you find it hard to start or do anything because you've lost your focus. Or if you are supposed to complete a project but you didn't, you start to feel bad about it and all you think is how irresponsible you are and that you are lazy, and you lack motivation. The point is, our brain shuts off from the outside world and relies on the negative emotions of fear, stress, and anger. Negative thoughts and emotions prevent us from seeing other options, solutions or choices that are around us.

What Can Positive Thinking do to your Brain?

Barbara Fredrickson also explains how positive thinking manifests in our brain. She explains with an experiment where research subjects are divided into five groups, and each group is shown a different video clip. The first group was shown clips that created feelings of joy whereas the second group was shown clips that created contentment, the third was the control group that had images of no significant emotions and were neutral whereas group four had clips that created fear and group five had clips that created the feelings of anger.

Participants were then asked to imagine themselves in situations that these same emotions would come about and write down their reactions to it. Participants that viewed images of fear and anger had the least responses or reactions whereas participants who saw joy and contentment had more reactions. The bottom line is, if you experience positive emotions you will see more possibilities in life. Positive emotions broaden our possibilities and thinking, thus opening up more options for us in facing issues, crisis, problems, and solutions and so on. In the next few chapters, we will discuss how we can work our mind to be more positive and look at things in a more positive perspective to enhance and give more value to our life, relationships, and goals. It is not as hard as it seems because all it takes is a little practice.

Have you seen the movie Inside Out?

If you did, then you will probably realize that being sad is a good thing- not always, but this emotion is there for a reason. When we talk about dealing with negativity, it doesn't necessarily mean being optimistic all the time, especially in the face of suffering.

Pain and sadness are just part of the complex human emotions all of us have, and it is just as important to feel pain and sadness, guilt and fear as this are all part and parcel of coping. Experiencing and processing negative emotions in a healthy way is a crucial part of personal growth.

There are two scenarios when people are confronted with negative situations. One, they either obsess over the problem or two, they numb their emotions. Either of these coping methods is not healthy, and it can create harmful patterns in our mind, over a period of time. Obsessing is deceptive because it feels as if you are thinking things through but to continuously obsess over a situation only reinforces the impact of the negative thoughts and emotions.

That said, numbing your emotions towards a pained situation isn't good either because it really is not possible to selectively numb out an emotion. Humans are so complex that our range of emotions does not enable us to directly shut down an emotion. If you somehow blot out anger, you'll blur out happiness and serenity too. Why? Because while you like being active and optimistic all the time, not showing anger to something that has hurt you or pained you or frustrated you, will make you feel more bitter eventually. Only because you weren't able to express your anger, the situation or the person related to this will not know how you feel. For example, if we use alcohol to numb our pain, we do not learn how to cope with sadness. We just develop another problem which is alcohol abuse.

If you are going through a pained time, then you need to develop healthy coping skills, and this involves recognizing the inevitability and necessity of some suffering and moving on from it. The process usually includes:

- Acknowledging your negative feelings and watch them with a non-judgmental attitude

- Recognize when they are triggered and assess your reactions when responding to this
- Understand that pain is just a catalyst for growth and resilience
- Practice forgiveness towards those who have pained you
- Express yourself in creative and healthy ways like painting or exercising
- Seek the support of others

Steps to deal with Negative thoughts and Events

Here are some tried and tested ways to overcome negative thoughts and events which you can try:

1. *Meditate or do yoga.*

Yoga helps take your focus away from your thoughts and bring attention to your breath. Yoga or meditation is very relaxing, and it helps ease one's mind. It also helps you stay present and focused on the moment that is happening.

2. *Smile.*

Pain and sadness can make it very hard to smile. While it does seem hard to smile when you aren't feeling so happy inside, you need to sometimes force this out of you. So try doing this in front of a mirror everyday or make a mental note to smile to the people you correspond with daily.

3. *Surround yourself with positive people.*

Surround yourself with friends and family that can give you constructive and loving feedback. Each time you feel you are going down into your negative spiral, call these people up and speak to them so they can put your focus back again to where it's needed to be at the time.

4. *Change your thoughts from negative to positive.*

Easier said than done, no doubt but you can turn any situation into a positive one. For example, if you have just started a new job you barely have enough experience of, instead of saying 'I'll take a long time to adjust or learn' just say 'I will take on any challenges because challenges excite me!'

5. *Don't wallow in self-pity. Take charge of your life*

You are the captain of your shop so do not make yourself a victim. There is always a way out of any situation so if it becomes to unbearable, then leave. Otherwise, you stay put and make the best of it and don't point fingers, blame, complain or whine.

6. *Volunteer*

Volunteering also takes the focus away. If you think you are in a bad situation, imagine the people who need food aid or money. Do something nice for someone else so volunteer at an organization or donate.

7. *Remember to keep moving forward*

We easily dwell on our mistakes and feel terrible for the way we acted. But you can't reverse the situation so instead of feeling sorry for yourself or beating yourself up over what you'd done, tell yourself that you'd made a mistake, you learned from it, and you want to move on.

8. *Listen to music*

One of the best ways to alleviate your mood especially in the morning is by listening to songs and singing in the shower! It doesn't matter if you remember the lyrics – a good happy song will put you in a good and happy mood.

9. *Be grateful*

Being grateful enables you to appreciate all the things you have. So be grateful every day.

10. *Read positive quotes.*

Just log into Pinterest, read positive quotes every day. Better yet, print out the ones that you like and stick in on your wall, your fridge or your computer.

Learn to Forgive Yourself

Just like negative emotions, failure is also good to experience because it only makes us stronger.

Yes! Failure is something that didn't kill you. You're still alive! So what doesn't kill you only makes you stronger. Why do you need experience failure? Nobody wants to experience failure but if you looked at the successful people in our generation today, or even the past- they all failed. They all made mistakes. They all went through trial and error. What sets them apart from the perennial failures? They didn't give up. They learnt from their mistakes. They had extreme passion, making them eager to keep on trying till they succeeded. Here's why you need to experience failure:

Without failure, you'd be sucked into a blissful feeling that nothing can go wrong and that everything you'd put into place will work exactly as how it should be

When something does go wrong, you are unable to cope with the change or adapt to create solutions.

Failure enables us to work on our flaws and it also allows us to right our wrongs. Failure also enables us upgrade or enhance or refine our work, technique and solutions

Failure also teaches us a lesson. It is our choice to learn from it or run from it

When we fail, it's easy to get discouraged and upset and we develop a sense of being afraid to fail again. In order to be successful in anything that we do, we just need to remind ourselves to let go of our pride and ego. Failure only makes us grow wiser, make us more adaptable and vivid to any possible scenarios that could happen. We are more prepared to face the same problem but at a different angle.

So how do you look at failure at a positive way? We need to redefine the way we view failure. The fear of failure is what stops many great individuals from creating something beneficial and meaningful in our world. The fear of failure is why we stop ourselves from living extraordinary lives.

The fear of failure is why we never submitted the novel we wrote, we never expressed our feelings to the people we love, never bungee jumped or telling someone how you really feel.

Daniel Epstein, founder of Unreasonable group stresses the point of re-branding the way we see failure. He suggests defining it as such:

"To Fail means "to not start doing something you believe in. To stop doing something you believe in just because it is hard. To ignore your gut instinct around what you believe is right and wrong."

In actual fact, many of the world's greatest philosophers, entrepreneurs, scientists and artisans have all expressed their thoughts on failure and how it has helped them overcome adversity and obstacles. All these perceptions tell us that fear of failure is evident in every human being but with passion and perseverance to achieve what you want will be the driving force in the determination between constant failure and success.

Hopefully, these quotes will give you a good perspective. After all, what better way to learn than to be inspired by some of the most successful people on earth?

Remembering that I'll be dead soon is the most important tool I've ever encountered to help me make the big choices in life. Because almost everything – all external expectations, all pride, all fear of embarrassment or failure – these things just fall away in the face of death, leaving only what is truly important. ~Steve Jobs

I've missed more than 9000 shots in my career. I've lost almost 300 games. 26 times, I've been trusted to take the game winning shot and missed. I've failed over and over and over again in my life. And that is why I succeed. ~Michael Jordan

Our doubts are traitors, and make us lose the good we oft might win, by fearing to attempt. ~William Shakespeare

For every failure, there's an alternative course of action. You just have to find it. When you come to a roadblock, take a detour. ~Mary Kay Ash

Failure is blindness to the strategic element in events; success is readiness for instant action when the opportune moment arrives. ~Newell D. Hillis

The only real failure in life is not to be true to the best one knows. ~Buddha

Success is often achieved by those who don't know that failure is inevitable. ~Coco Chanel

Steps to Overcome Failure

Highly successful people are the ones who have failed the most. We only hear about their successes but never the trials and tribulations and obstacles that they had to go through. Setbacks and failures are part of life and nobody is perfect. Yes we fall into hard times at some point in our lives but what this is all a lesson to us. If we can manage it effectively, then no matter what comes our way in the future, we can overcome it. Here are four steps that can help you turn any negative experience into a positive one:

- **Failure is part of the road to success**

When times get tough, the tough get going. It is frustrating to hear people tell us to be positive when we are faced with adversity but this doesn't mean we have to be smiling all the time or be happy all the time. Staying positive is knowing that despite your setback, you can bounce back again. Staying positive is learning and growing and evolving. Understand that setbacks aren't the end of the road; rather it is carving a step in our journey to succeed. When life hits you with a setback, its okay to be sad and frustrated and upset- but we should never stay down.

- **Blow your Steam off**

When you hit a setback or a failure, your mind gets clouded. You worked so hard to get to this point, only to fail. If you have come to this point, take a step back and evaluate your work. Take some time off to clear your head and accept your mistakes. Once you have done this, you will begin to accept what has happened and how it happened or why it happened. This emotional state will eventually evaporate and then you can go back to focus on the work at hand.

- **Be Honest**

Being brutally honest to ourselves in the midst of a failure is a trait of success. Most people do not want to admit their mistake or admit that it is their own fault that all these negative scenarios have happened. The thing is, part of being positive is also about being responsible and being accountable to ourselves and the mistakes we have made. We need to do this because this is how we learn. Albert Einstein once said that it is crazy to keep doing the same thing over and over again and expecting different results. That is why learning from our mistakes is a crucial part of moving on and part of learning. If we do not learn from our mistakes, we are doomed to be repeating them again and again and again.

- **Move Forward**

We need to move forward each time we fail. When we fail, we fail forward which means learning from our setbacks and then, making the necessary adjustments until we reach success. You have come so far, do not give up. So each change we make, each person we meet and every tiny bit of information we learn all combines to create a different outcome for us to learn from.

Obstacles are inevitable in life but there are always two ways of handling them. While they may block your focus out temporarily, our perseverance is the element that determines whether we fall back or move forward. As we get more and more efficient in the journey of positive thinking, we will enable ourselves to always see the positive side of things even in the most darkest of situations or the hardest of times.

Surrounding yourself with Positive People

No doubt that people have a huge impact on your life. According to Jim Rohn, American entrepreneur and motivation speaker, we all spend our time with an average of five people. With this in mind, think about who these 5 people are and how they impact your life.

Some people, including your friends whom you've known for a long time, can be parasites. These parasites suck out your energy and happiness and even your resources.

So what makes someone a 'good' person you can spend your time with? What are the benefits of surrounding yourself with self-disciplined people?

Your GOOD Category

The people around you can be good in so many ways. This doesn't mean that they go to church every Sunday. It's more like feeding the poor, looking after abandon dogs or something simple like encouraging you to hit the gym more often. These people can be your friends, your family, your co-workers and even some acquaintances.

In essence, good people are productive people. They have a lot of good traits in them that inspire and motivate you too.

It is also important to note too much of something good can also inhibit your growth. You need diversity and healthy arguments and discussions along the way. Always be eager to learn new knowledge and look at different perspectives from your peers.

Think About How You Interact with People

Time for a little exercise. Write down the names of the five people you usually spend time with. Then, write down the qualities you see in them. Think about how they positively or negatively affect you. Are you happy around them? Do they make you feel like you got what it takes to reach your goals? Do they support you? If your list has more positives than negatives, then you probably have the good people around you.

You want to surround yourself with people who make you happy, with those that make you feel alive, the people who help you when you are in need and those that make you feel safe- they are the ones who genuinely care and are worth keeping in your life.

The key here is to finding what is good for you because what is good for you may be different for someone else.

So how do you do that?

Your vibe is what will attract the people around you. When you give off good vibes, good vibes will follow you. You will also feel less stressed and find joy even in the most simplest things like the blue sky or a scoop of vanilla ice cream.

So train your mind to not think negatively and try to see the positive side of things. It is ok to feel sadness and grief and bitterness when things don't go the way you want or something bad happens but if you start building a home in the negativity scene, it'll be harder for you to leave it.

Today, make a commitment to start spending more time with the good people in your life.

Benefits of surrounding yourself with Positive People
1. You Do not get into needless battles

Thoughts become things- you've heard it before. But some of these things are also feelings and feelings are energy. The feelings of happiness, sadness, gratitude, confidence are all energy- negative and positive. When you surround yourself with positive people, you eliminate negative energy, thus eliminate unnecessary conflicts.

You get to live in the feeling of gratitude more frequently

People who are happy will genuinely be happy for you when you make it big or achieve your goal. Surrounding yourself with unsuccessful people and then talking about your successes will only remind these people of what they don't have. By contrast, surrounding yourself with people that have more than what you have you will make you feel more gratitude frequently. Gratitude is the attitude that brings success.

For example, if you achieved your goal in achieving a healthy, physically toned body, you're not going to be telling this to someone who is overweight (by choice) right? Because that person will only think you are bragging and wont share in your good fortune.

2. You get to be someone you've never been

In order to do something you have never done before, you need to stop caring about what people think of you. You need to realize that you cannot be doing the same things you have done if you want to become someone better. Surrounding yourself with people who want to achieve the same goal as you can make you do things you otherwise will not do. Successful people recognize that change is inevitable and that it must take place. Unsuccessful people will begrudge the changes in you whereas successful people will be glad that it happened and welcome it.

Chapter 5: Building and Mastering Emotions

Being aware of our emotions also means knowing that our emotions can drive our behavior and impact those around us, either positively or negatively. It also means we have the ability to manage these emotions, that of our own and that of others, especially at pressuring and stressful times.

The Five Categories of Emotional Intelligence (EQ)

When it comes to Emotional Intelligence, there are five categories that becomes a focus.

1. **Self-awareness.**

Having self-awareness means having the ability to recognize an emotion as and when it occurs and it is the key to your EQ. In order to develop self-awareness, a person needs to tune into their own true feelings, evaluating them and subsequently managing them.

In self-awareness, the important elements are:

- Recognizing our own own emotions and its effects
- Having a level of confidence and sureness of your capabilities and your self-worth

2. **Self-regulation.**

When we experience emotions, we often have little control over our actions when we first feel these emotions. One thing we can control however is how long these emotions last. To control how long certain emotions last, especially negative ones, certain methods are used to lessen the effects of these emotions such as anxiety, anger and even depression. These methods include reinventing a scenario in a much positive manner such as through taking a long walk, saying a prayer and even meditating.

Self-regulation includes:
- Innovation which means open to new ideas
- Adaptability to handle change and be flexible
- Trustworthiness referring to the ability to keep to standards of integrity and honesty
- Taking responsibility, conscientiousness of our own actions
- Self-control to prevent disruptive impulses

3. **Motivation**

Having motivation is what keeps us going to accomplish our tasks and goals and to maintain an air of positivity. With practice and with effort, we can all program our minds to be more positive although as human beings, it is also good to be negative at times. This does not mean having negative thoughts are bad, but these thoughts need to be kept in check as they cause more harm than good. Whenever you feel like you have negative feelings, you can also reprogram them to be more positive or at least to pick out the positive aspects of the situation, the silver lining which will help you be more focused in solving the problem.

Motivation is made up of:
- Having the sense of achievement drive, to constantly strive to improve and meet a level of excellence.
- Having the commitment to align your individual, group or organizational goals
- Having the initiative to act on available opportunities
- Having the optimism to pursue your goals persistently and objectively, despite the setbacks and obstacles.

4. **Empathy**

Empathy is the ability to recognize how people would feel towards a certain scenario, thing or person. Having this ability is crucial to success both in career as with life. The more you can decipher the feelings of people, the better you can manage the thoughts and approaches you send them. Empathetic people are excellent at:

- Recognizing, anticipating and meeting a person's needs
- Developing the needs of other people and bolstering their individual abilities
- Taking advantage of diversity by cultivating opportunities among different people
- Developing political awareness by understanding the current emotional state of people and fostering powerful relationships
- Focusing on identifying feelings and wants of other people

5. **Social skills.**

Developing good interpersonal skills is imperative as well if you want a successful life and a successful career. In our world today when plenty of thing are digitized, social skills seem to be an afterthought. People skills are more relevant and sought-after then before especially since now you also need a high EQ understand, negotiate and empathize with others especially if you deal and interact with different people on a daily basis. Among the most useful skills are:

- Influence to effectively wield persuasive tactics
- Communication to send our clear and concise messages
- Leadership to inspire and guide people and groups.
- Change catalyst in kick-starting and managing change
- Managing conflicting situations which includes the ability to negotiate, understand and resolve disagreements

- To bond and nurture meaningful and instrumental relationships
- Teamwork, cooperation and collaboration in meeting shared goals
- Creating a synergetic group to work towards collective goals.

Creating a Balance with Emotional Awareness

As a human being, emotions and feelings make up every aspect of our existence. Managing them and keeping them balanced will help us reach our maximum potential in life, at work and especially in our relationships. As we know by now, having good emotional balance leads us towards better physical and mental health, making life happier.

When our emotional well-being is disrupted, this will result in the opposite. Our physical health will decline, we will start having digestive problems, lack of energy and sleep issues. People with emotional distress often exhibit low self-esteem, they are self-critical and pessimistic. They always need to assert themselves through their behavior. They are overly worried, get afraid very fast and they are focused on the past.

- Connection between our Thoughts and Feelings

Thoughts determine our feelings and they are nothing more than firing the neurons in our body. Our thoughts also generate feelings, making our body release additive natural substances such as cortisol and adrenaline.

The connection between the body and the mind is extremely vivid and strong, strong enough that the mental and physical state sends positive and negative vibes both ways. The feelings we experience depends on our thought, combined with our attitudes and actions.

Emotions are part of our daily life and we experience this everyday. What we want is to strike a balance in our emotions, thoughts and feelings to ensure that they do not adversely affect our daily tasks and cause us stress.

- **Creating Emotional Balance**

So how we do create emotional balance? Emotional balance is the ability to maintain equilibrium and flexibility between the mind and body when we are faced with changes or challenges. Here are some ways that you can create emotional balance:

1. **Accept your emotions**

Many of our mental, emotional and physical problems stem from our inability to express ourselves emotionally. When we experience an emotional distraught, we smother it in the comforts of eating, sleeping, sweating it out, sucking it up, it is swept under a rug, we bury it, project it elsewhere, meditate even all in the hopes of suppressing our emotions instead of actually dealing with it by accepting that this is what we are going through right not. The key here is to allow ourselves unconditional permission to feel- to cry when we want to, to feel anger when we are angry, sadness when we grief and so on. Let your guard down either when you are alone or with someone you trust and just focus on the feeling and situation. Experience and immerse yourself in this feeling so you can comprehend better why it hurts and what you will be doing to remedy the situation once you've accepted and acknowledge these feelings.

2. **Express yourself**

Expressing yourself is important. There are many ways to express oneself and usually when we experience a feeling, we react by crying, shouting, throwing things. But to identify with ourselves and be able to manage our emotions properly, we can also express ourselves through more positive ways. Some people like reading as it provides an escape into a different world. Some people express themselves through art or music. Whatever it is that you do, make sure you stay connected to discover more about yourself, your identity and also the person you want to become.

3. Don't shove your feelings

Sometimes, it is easy to shove our feelings and not think about it, especially painful and scary memories. But as we all know, stuffing your memories and feelings will only make things worse for you. While it is hard to address your fears and sadness, rage and anger, once you actually dive into it, you will find that it will become easier to face your fears and eventually, the choppy waters will become calmer.

Be accepting your past and dealing with it in a more emotional state, you ultimately will lead a harmonious life. Always allow yourself to feel because your reactions to these different feelings would be in a more stable way rather than an overreaction.

4. See the world in a positive light

It is easier said than done, we know. In a world full of hatred, sadness, grief, war, crime, unfairness- it is a threat to our emotional health. You tend to develop low self-esteem and start asking yourself if you are worth it, if you can get through it, if you are doing things right and all these thinking steers you towards making more mistakes and missteps. Rather than having emotional self-doubt, take action to develop a prerogative of seeing the world in a more positive light.

Do not feel responsible for the bad things that happen which is not caused by you is a good start. Have compassion in yourself and practice mindfulness and accept that occasional lapses and failures are just part of being human.

5. Get a grip on your mind

The way we think causes us emotional distress- this probably is not news to you.

We all have this tendency into overthinking and these thoughts that do not serve you or give you any positivity is just setting you up for emotional distress. So get a grip on your mind- do not let it wander to much especially when you start overthinking.

6. **Practice Yoga and Mindfulness**

Doing yoga on a daily basis does help in your mental health- it helps by increasing your confidence in your abilities and it also helps you make better, definitive decisions.

You also learn to not be so self-criticizing. Yoga, practiced on a daily basis can help get rid of negative energy within you and help you work your way towards mental clarity and vital energy.

Not only that, the breathing that is practiced in yoga helps you relax better, make you calmer especially if your mind is racing and it also helps you to refine your feelings.

Breathing correctly helps you get rid of stress and anxiety as well.

Conclusion

While emotional balance is vital, just remember that it is alright to have emotional imbalance so do not beat yourself up over it and overthink things. However, do not neglect this imbalance. If you feel you are emotionally imbalanced, do something about it either talk to someone you trust, meet a therapist or just find a positive way to express your emotions and feelings. Live a life without or little regrets.

Chapter 6: Practical steps for Becoming self compassionate

Self-compassion is necessary for a healthy relationship, healthy mind and healthy body. How we interact with people and how we think affects how our body responds too. Self-compassion is the practice of goodwill and not good feelings. To practice self-compassion, we have first and foremost, change the way we think and perceive things. We also need a little bit of faith and believe in ourselves, in our strengths, in the way our life is heading, our goals and our priorities.

In this chapter, we will look at:

- the power of faith and believe in changing our perceptions
- practising creative visualization
- Practising affirmations

- **Faith & Believe**

When someone says 'Have faith' this depends on what you view or think what faith is. For many people, faith can be many different things and in all honesty, there's no right or wrong.

Conventionally, a lot of people associate faith with spirituality or the faith in God and that's not wrong either but like mentioned above, the very fact that people have different perspectives of what faith is is a good thing! It is quite enlightening and helpful to plenty of individuals that faith has different meanings as it can help different people make clearer sense of the various spectrums of life.

Here's a quick guideline to what faith means:

- **Faith**

Faith can mean faith in a supreme being, in God. But psychologists of religion would say that this is more of belief. Faith, in a more naturalistic and psychological sense, is really about the innate sense to search for meaning, purpose, and significance. Every human person has a strong sense that there is more than what meets the eye. In other words, there is something more than just 'me' and as human beings, we all discover what this might be- some of us go all out while some of us are content with the information we have at the moment.

All of us human beings seek out to find the deeper meaning, purpose and significance that exist in our lives, in our relationships and all the things that occur around us. This is the very basic striving of faith and the universal role it plays in our lives.

Wikipedia describes faith as a trust or confidence on a person, element or thing. Faith also is connected to the observation of an obligatory process that creates loyalty or even fidelity to a person, a promise or engagement. Faith is also a belief that is not based on facts and proof and faith can also mean loyalty to a system of religious belief.

While we think that only people that belief in divine intervention or God seem to have faith, the thing is even atheists have this kind of faith- a belief or trust or confidence. Everyone has the gift of faith- some of us have strong faith while some of us have weaker faith, but it really depends on the context we talk about.

- Belief

This brings us to the next element- belief. Belief is a representation of truth claims that you make on your spiritual journey. Beliefs are what tell you what is true and what is not true, and this is based on your experiences to satisfy your sense of faith. Your beliefs are what your hold to be true in your journey to satisfy your faith by engaging in various spiritual pursuits such as pilgrimage.

- **The Value of Faith**

While we all like to think we have faith (and high levels of it) the truth is, the value of our faith only grows when we are faced with troubling times. Many people believe that their faith value is determined by the evidence of things or successful moments or achievements in life. But the value of faith only increases as we grow older, as we experience more and more things in life, some good and some bad. Our faith becomes more valuable as we go through the trials and testaments of life and its heartaches. It is only during these times that you truly understand the depth and strength of a person's faith.

- **The Difference between Faith & Belief**

Probably by reading this now, you'd come to deduce that faith and belief are not the same things. In fact, in most cases, faith and belief are entirely the opposite of each other. Confusion between these two elements is tested when you face a crisis. While you may be searching for faith in something at a moment of crisis, you may be only pulling out the various beliefs that you have.

So the question is, who are you if not for your convictions?

If you have gone through a terrible crisis in life, you are probably still trying to figure it all out. Some people take years to understand why what happened to them, happened. Many people, especially those who are religious, feel the need to leave their faith in God because they believe that God has abandoned them.

But the questions are, were you abandoned by God or were you abandoned by your beliefs?

- **Belief as a product of the Mind**

A negative mind is already at a disadvantage but even a healthy mind can run into its own set of problems. For the enabled mind, a person may think that because they pray to God, all their prayers will be answered and that God is just and he will set things right. The positive mind will say that if we hold on to our beliefs strongly, God listens and will favor us.

But what is it that we believe in? Our beliefs are rooted in our culture and our upbringing. This is the first thing that separates our faith from our belief. Oftentimes, what we belief in may directly contradict everything else we know to be true and right. It can be universally acknowledged that we arrive at the crossroads of faith and belief when we go through a life-threatening crisis ourselves and when this happens, we end up changing our stronghold beliefs.

Changing our minds to adapt to crises is to change some part or elements of our beliefs. It is perfectly normal to shift our beliefs because our beliefs are modeled on personal and communal experience. A belief can necessarily be not true even when it has been handed down to us. In other words, a belief is not necessarily the only truth.

- **Belief is a product of the mind, faith is not**

Faith is the product of the spirit. Our mind also has a tendency to interfere with the process of faith rather than contributing it. To have confidence in the most depressing of times will require us to quiet the mind because the mind can run amok when we let it, especially when we have every negative thought clouding our mind.

Faith comes in when our beliefs run aground. Be wary that our beliefs can sway our spirit. Think of Galileo and how everyone thought the world was flat until he came around to prove that the world was indeed round. The belief that we humans have held for centuries can come and go over the course of a millennium.

- **Beliefs come and go**

But our faith is not as fickle as our belief. True faith is not a statement of our beliefs, but it is a state of being. Faith is trusting beyond all reasonable doubt and beyond all evidence that you have not been abandoned. Faith is achieved through commitment and to commit to faith is not the same thing as committing to a series of beliefs. When we are in the moment of crisis, faith tells us it doesn't matter whether its God or circumstances. To not know in the perspective of faith is to remain humble and open to learning. When faith does not fill in the cracks in a crisis, then fear will. Therefore, faith is an attitude that we create where it is the acceptance of not knowing. Unknowing is what creates faith.

Practicing Creative Visualization to Encourage Self-Compassion

Creative visualization is a mental technique that harnesses our imagination to make our goals and dreams a reality. When used the right way, creative visualization has been proven to improve the lives of the people who have used it, and it also increases the success and prosperity rate of the individual. Creative visualization unleashes a power that can alter your social and living environment and circumstances, it causes beneficial events to happen, attracts positivity in work, life, relationships, and goals.

Creative visualization is not a magic potion. It uses the cognitive processes of our mind to purposely generate an array of visual mental imagery to create beneficial physiological, psychological or social effects such as increasing wealth, healing wounds to the body or alleviating psychological issues such as anxiety and sadness. This method uses the power of the mind to attract good energy and really, it is the magic potion behind every success.

Mostly, a person needs to visualize an individual event or situation or object or desire to attract it into their lives. This is a process that is similar to daydreaming. It only uses the natural process of the power of our mind to initiate positive thoughts and natural mental laws. Successful people like Oprah and Tiger Woods and Bill Gates use this technique, either consciously or unconsciously, attracting success and positive outcomes into their lives by visualizing their goals as already attained or accomplished.

- **The Power of Thoughts and Creative Visualization**

So how does this work and why is it so important to us?

Well, our mind is a powerful thing. With only the power of our mind, we can reach amazing success, or we can also spiral out of control. It swings both ways. Our subconscious mind accepts the ideals and thoughts that we often repeat, and when our mind accepts it, then your mindset also changes accordingly, and this influences your habits and actions. Again, a domino effect happens where you end up meeting new people or getting into situations or circumstances that lead you to your goal. Our thoughts come with a creative power that can mold our life and attract whatever we think about.

Remember the saying that goes 'mind over matter?' When we set our mind to do it, our body does what our mind tells us. Our thoughts travel from mind, body, and soul but believe it or not; it can travel from one mind to another because it is unconsciously picked up by the people you meet with every day and usually, most of the people you end up meeting are the ones who can help you achieve your goals.

You probably think and repeat certain thoughts everyday pretty often, and you probably do this consciously or unconsciously. You probably have focused your thoughts on your current situation or environment and subsequently, create and recreate the same events and circumstances regularly. While most of our lives are somewhat routine, we can always change these thoughts by visualizing different circumstances and situations, and in a way, create a different reality for you to focus on new goals and desires.

- **Changing Your Reality**

Honestly, though, you can change your 'reality by changing your thoughts and mental images. You aren't creating magic here; all you are doing is harnessing the natural powers and laws that inhibit each and every one of us. The thing that separates normal, average folk with wildly successful people is that the successful ones have mastered their thoughts and mental images while the rest of us are still learning or trying to cope. Changing your thoughts and attitude changes and reshapes your world.

Take for example you plan on moving into a larger apartment and instead of wallowing in self-pity such as the lack of money, do this instead- alter your thoughts and attitude and visualize yourself living in a larger apartment. It isn't difficult to do because it's exactly like daydreaming.

- **Overcoming Limited Thinking**

You may think daydreaming about positive things and money and success and great relationships are nothing but child's play but in fact, creative visualization can do wonders. Though that, it may be hard for different individuals to immediate alter their thoughts. Limits to this positive thinking are within us and not the power of our mind- we control it.

It might sound like its easy to change the way you think, but the truth is, it takes a lot of effort on your side to alter your thoughts at least in the immediate future. But never for a second doubt that you can't. Anything that you put your mind to work on, it can be done.

We often limit ourselves due to our beliefs and our thoughts and to the life we know. So the need to be open-minded is an integral part of positive thinking. The bigger we dare to think, the higher and great our changes, possibilities and opportunities. Limitations are created within our minds, and it is up to use to rise above all these obstacles.

Of course, it takes time to change the way we think and see things and broaden our horizons, but small demonstrations of changing our minds and the way we think will yield bigger results in due time.

- **Guidelines for Creating Visualization**

Concise Guidelines for Creative Visualization:

Step 1: Define your goal.

Step 2: Think, meditate and listen to your instinct, ensure that this is the goal you want to attain

Step 3: Ascertain that you only want good results from your visualization, for you and for others around you.

Step 4: Be alone at a place that you will not be disturbed. Be alone with your thoughts.

Step 5: Relax your body and your mind

Step 6: Rhythmically breathe deeply several

Step 7: Visualize your goal by giving it a clear and detailed mental image

Step 8: Add desire and feelings into this mental image- how you would feel etc

Step 9: Use all your five senses of sight, hearing, touch, taste and smell

Step 10: Visualize this at least twice a day for at least 10 minutes each time

Step 11: Keep visualizing this day after day with patience, hope and faith

Step 12: Always keep staying positive in your feelings, thoughts and words

Staying positive can be easy, it is all about training your mind. When you do feel doubts, and negative thoughts arise, replace them with positive thoughts. Also remember to keep an open mind because opportunities come in various ways so when you see it, you can take advantage of them. Every morning, or each time you conclude your visualization session, always end it with this 'Let everything happen in a favorable way for everyone and everything involved.'

Creative visualization will open doors but it takes time and whenever you feel you are in a position of advantage, take action. Do not be passive or wait for things to fall on your lap. Perhaps you've met someone who can put yours in a position of advantage to reach your goal or perhaps you've landed a job that has the possibility of enabling you to travel. All these things come into your life, and if you have an open mind, you can see the possibilities more vividly.

When you use the power of imagination for you and the people around you, always do it for good. Never try creative visualization to obtain something forcibly that belongs to others (like someone else's husband or wife or a managerial position someone else rightfully achieved but you want as well). Also, don't harm the environment.

Most visualized goals happen in a natural and gradual manner, but there can be times that can happen in a sudden and expected manner too. Be realistic with your goals, though. Don't visualize a unicorn and expect it to turn up. If money is what you desire, you know that it just will not drop from the sky. You may or may not win it in the lottery. But the chances or possibilities are higher when you go through life with a new job, or you get a promotion, or you end up making a business deal.

It is always better to think and visualize what you actually want because you do not want to attract situations that are negative, in your quest to fulfill your goals and desires.

Using Affirmations

Affirmations have helped many people make significant changes in their lives and the people around them. Do they work for everyone? Why do some people have achieved success using this technique but some people do not get anything from it?

- **What are Affirmations?**

Affirmations are positive and direct statements that help an individual overcome self-sabotaging and negative thoughts. It helps a person visualize and believe in their goals, dreams, and abilities. In other words, you are affirming to yourself and helping yourself make positive changes to your life goals. Affirmations have the power to work because it can program a person's mind into believing a concept. The mind is known not to know the difference between what is real or fantasy. That is why when you watch a movie; you tend to empathize with the characters on the screen even though you know it's just a movie. But as soon as you leave the cinema, you are back into reality but can't help feel sorry or happy for the characters.

There are both positive and negative affirmations and some of these affirmations such as being told you are smart when you were a child or being told that you are clumsy can stick with us in both our conscious or unconscious mind. When we face failure, we tend to over-calculate the risks we are taking and work out the worst possible scenario which is usually the emotional equivalent of our parents or guardian deserting us.

We imagine an entirely dreadful scenario in our minds that we convince ourselves that trying to change isn't a good thing at all. Thus, it makes us lose out on opportunities for success and then when we actually do fail (because our mind is already convinced we'll fail anyway) the whole experience of affirmation that we give ourselves is that we are not cut out for success, or it is not in our karma to succeed, and then, we settle.

If a negative belief is firmly rooted in our subconscious mind, then it will have the ability to override any positive affirmation even when we aren't aware of it.

This is one of the reasons why people do not believe in positive affirmations because it doesn't seem to be working. Their negative patterns are so high it just knocks out the sun!

So how do we add affirmations into our daily life and how can we make them prevail above our negative thinking? Here are some steps to follow:

Making Affirmations Work for You

Step 1- On a day that you are alone and not busy or distracted (if you don't have a time like this, then make one) list down all your negative qualities. Include any criticism that others have made of you and those that you have been holding onto. Remember that we all have flaws so do not judge. By acknowledging your mistakes, you can then move forward and work on your flaws, and you can make a shift in your life. When you write these down, take note to see if you are holding any grudges along the way or holding on to it. For example, do you feel tightness or dread in your heart?

Step 2- Begin to write out an affirmation on the positive aspect of your self-assessment. Use powerful statement words to beef up this assessment. Instead of saying 'I am worthy' say 'I am extremely cherished and remarkable.'

Step 3- Practice every day reading this affirmation loudly for five minutes at least three times a day in the morning, afternoon and at night before going to sleep. You can do this while shaving or putting your make up on, or when you are fixing yourself a cup of tea or if you are in the shower. At best, look in the mirror, so you look at yourself and repeat these positive statements. You can also write these affirmations in your notebook at any time you feel like it. Take note of how your writing changes over time. If we do not like something, often writing this down will encompass using smaller handwriting but if we right in big and bold letterings, we are increasing the affirmation of this. This is really a mindfulness journey to get to the agenda of positive affirmation.

Step 4- To enhance the impact, do body movements such as placing your hand on your heart when you felt uncomfortable writing out a negative criticism of yourself in Step 1. As you work on reprogramming your mind to alter it from the concept of affirmation to a real and definite personification of the quality that you see.

Step 5- Get someone to help you repeat your affirmations. This can be a friend or a gym coach or just about anyone that you feel safe with. For example, if they are saying that you are cherished and remarkable, and then connect this statement with your situations such as 'excellent colleague' or 'good fathering.' If you are not comfortable with doing this with someone, then look at your reflection in the mirror and reinforce your positive message.

Affirmations can be an incredibly powerful tool that can help you change your state of mind, alleviate your mood and more importantly, ingrain the changes your desire into your life. But for all of this to happen, you first need to identify the negative and the work on getting rid of them in your life.

Examples of Positive Affirmation

Here are some examples of positive affirmations that you can use to relate to the various areas of your development:

- I know, accept and am true to myself
- I believe in myself and have confidence in my decisions
- I eat a balanced diet, exercise regularly and get plenty of rest
- I always learn from my mistakes
- I know I am capable of anything and can accomplish anything I set my mind to
- I have flaws and I am not perfect but that's ok because I am human
- I never, ever give up

- I can adapt and accept what I have no control over
- I make the best of every situation
- I always look at the bright side of life
- I enjoy life to the fullest
- I stand up for what I believe in, my morals and my values
- I treat others with respect and recognize their individuality
- I can make a difference
- I can practice understanding, patience and compassions
- I am always up to learn new things and be open-minded
- I live in the moment and learn from my past and prepare for my future

These are just some of the positive affirmations that you can use to be optimistic and pursue a fulfilling and happy mindset. Have fun in creating your own affirmations or tailor the above to suit your needs and situation. Most of the affirmations above can be used daily to uplift, inspire and motivate you and those around you.

Mindfulness Meditation for Self-Compassion

Have you thought about meditation or have you done meditation before? Meditation does wonders to your body, mind and soul. When it comes to practising self-compassion, mindful meditation helps you incorporate this into your daily life more frequently. Keep in mind that mindful meditation isn't only helpful for self-compassion but it also helps us deal with the negativity that we face when we want to practice self-compassion.

Exercise 1 – Mindful Breathing

Breathing is an essential part of the meditative experience, so it is only natural that we should

exercise this too. Whenever you meditate, you're breathing mindfully when you focus on each purposeful breath that goes in and out of your body. Mindful breathing doesn't just have to happen when you're meditating, it can be done anywhere and at any time whether you're sitting, standing or just walking about. Make it a habit to breathe mindfully and you'll find it much easier to do so during your meditation sessions.

1. Start by bringing your attention and focus to your breathing.
2. Breathe in slowly for approximately 3 seconds, and then release that breathe slowly, counting to 3 seconds again.
3. During this exercise, you should focus and be thinking of nothing else except your breathing. Do not think about the tasks you need to do, or a meeting that is coming up at work. Think about nothing but your breathing in and out, counting the seconds as you do.
4. Concentrate on the air that is filling your lungs as you breathe in, the way it makes your body feel, and when you release your breathe, imagine all the stress and the tension leaving your body as you do.

You can do this for 1-2 minutes at a time throughout the day, several times a day and you're already on your way towards improving each meditation session when you get better at learning to control your breathing.

Exercise 2 – Awareness

When you meditate, you learn to become more aware of your body, your mind and your thoughts, aware of what is happening all around you when your eyes are closed because your other senses become heightened when your eyes are shut. Being mindfully aware helps you sharpen your focus and remain alert to not just your surroundings, but your thoughts as well. For example, if you were mindfully aware about your thoughts, you will have better control when it comes to keeping any negative thought or emotion at bay.

Exercising your awareness throughout the day will help sharpen your alertness towards everything around you. Not just around you, but within you too. Beginners often find focusing on awareness to be a struggle in the beginning, because its so easy to let our thoughts drift and get distracted by everything else. Training yourself to be more aware will help you better connect your mind and body during your meditation sessions, so it's a good idea to practice these throughout the day to help you sharpen your focus and cultivate a heightened sense of awareness.

1. Start by choosing an activity or an object to focus on. Pick something that you would normally do without thinking twice about it, like opening the door or getting dressed in the morning for example.
2. Once you've got your object or activity, start to really, actively pay attention to what you're doing. If you're opening the door, concentrate on it. Reach for the doorknob and be aware of how it feels in your hand, and the motion of pulling the door towards you or away from you. Stop and appreciate how lucky you are to be healthy and fit enough to walk out your front door with a destination and a purpose in mind.
3. When you're getting dressed in the morning, focus and be aware of what you're doing instead of just going through the motions. Concentrate on how the fabric of your clothes feel in your hand, and even stop to appreciate how fortunate you are to be able to have a selection of clothes to choose from as you go through your closet looking for something to wear.
4. Before you eat, be aware of the food that is in front of you, how good it smells, the shapes, the colors. As you take each bite and begin to chew, be aware of how the food tastes and you take each bite with purpose.

Eventually, being mindfully aware is something that will come much easier, and the more you practice the easier you will find it is to concentrate on what you're doing or thinking without becoming easily distracted by other thoughts around you.

Exercise 3 – Mental Focus

Successful meditation involves being able to concentrate and not let your thoughts get easily distracted, which means you're going to need to work on improving your focus. Exercises to improve your focus are simple enough, here's what you can do:

1. Pick an object to focus on and place it in front of you.
2. When you're ready, set a timer and start to focus on the object and nothing else.
3. Concentrate on that object and keep staring at it for as long as you can.
4. When your mind begins to wander, stop and make a note of how long you managed to concentrate on that object before your mind started to drift.
5. Next round, do the same thing but try to go for a longer time this time around, aiming to beat your previous record.

Gradually, you should be able to focus on the object in front of you for longer periods of time before you find yourself getting distracted. The longer you can focus on the object, the better your focusing abilities will become.

PART IV

Chapter 1: What is Holding You Back

The first half of this book focused on the negative aspects of clutter and how removing unnecessary items from your life can be cathartic in so many ways. The goal of all of this was to begin getting things done in your life. This includes all aspects of a person's personal and professional life. Honestly, decluttering was just the first step. It was a way to clear up our minds and reduce distractions. After doing this, it is time to start moving forward and getting things done in our lives. Now that our physical and mental spaces are clear, what else can we focus on? The goal of this chapter is to present some of the biggest challenges to getting things done.

Why People Procrastinatn

Procrastination is something many people in our society suffer with. It is the purposeful and unnecessary delay of actions or decisions. Why do something now when you can just do it tomorrow? Well, because you never know what tomorrow will bring. Other challenges will arise, distractions will come up, and you will continue to load up your plate because you refuse to take things off of it. Since you are making the excuse today for waiting until tomorrow, what is stopping you from making the same excuse tomorrow, or the next day and the next day?

Imagine being at a buffet and loading up your plate. When you go to sit down, you decide not to eat much of the food because you want it later. Instead, you go and grab another plate to fill up and bring back to the table. Now, you have two plates to finish, and you have no idea how you will do it. Eventually, the restaurant is about to close, and you don't have the time or space to finish everything. You will most likely waste a large portion of the food. This is what procrastination looks like in life. You keep pushing things back until you become overloaded, overwhelmed, and very close to the deadline, if you even make it at all.

Procrastination is one of the worst enemies of getting things done. It really has no value, except for the fact that some people thrive on making quick deadlines. However, you will also be more likely to make big mistakes. You will never be able to complete the work to your full potential because so many things will be missed. Even if they're minor, they still add up.

Procrastination leads to so many missed opportunities too. Several people do not pursue their goals because they put them off for too long. Eventually, they get to the point where they lose interest or become too involved in other things to where they no longer have time.

People assume that procrastination has everything to do with will power. While this can be a major reason, for sure, it is not the only one that exists. There are many deeper reasons for why people put things off. There are some psychological aspects that are at play. For example, anxiety and fear of failure will terrify people into paralysis. Nobody wants to fail, and if they start something, failure is a huge possibility. As a result, we delay starting anything. At least then, we can save face a little bit.

When our motivation to complete a task outweighs the negative aspects, then there's a strong chance we will still finish it. However, if the negative aspects outweigh our own motivation, then we will put off pursuing a goal if we even do so at all. The following are some other factors that keep up from moving forward. If we follow these, we will always procrastinate.

Abstract Goals

If a person has a vague or abstract goal, then they are more likely to procrastinate. They are not excited enough about it. In fact, they might not even know what the goal is, as there is no clear definition. For example, making a promise to get fit is an abstract goal. It is a simple statement with no real substance. What are the chances you will get fit if you have no actual plan in place for doing so? Furthermore, what does "get fit" even mean to? Does it mean losing a certain amount of weight, gaining muscle, looking slimmer, having more energy, or a combination of all? Honestly, you are not even giving yourself a chance to obtain this goal, as you will just put it off until you forget about it.

A more solid goal would be, "I will lose 15 pounds within two months and be able to run six miles by then." This is a concrete goal with real values and end results. From here, you can create specific action steps to get there. For example, losing two pounds and increasing your run mileage by one every week. Once you create real goals with a legitimate plan, then you are more likely to not put things off.

Not Having Foreseeable Rewards

Many individuals put things off because they see no actual rewards in the near future. For example, a teenager may not attend college because he or she cannot fathom waiting four years or more to get a degree in something that might make them money. In addition, the money will not come right away, which is another deterrent.

People often want immediate pleasure rather than long-term success. This can be seen in people neglecting to create savings or investment accounts. They do not want money later; they want it now. As a result, they delay setting up one of these essential accounts because they can't see the benefits they will create in the future.

This same mindset can apply to punishments, as well. The farther into the future a punishment is, the less likely it will motivate someone to take action. If you are studying for a final exam in college and it is months away, you are not that concerned about it, because even if you fail, it will be a while until that actually happens.

A Disconnect from Our Future Selves

People tend to procrastinate because they cannot comprehend a connection between their present and future selves. They believe the two individuals are mutually exclusive for some reason and don't realize that they are creating their future person by the actions you take today.

A person may delay starting a healthy diet because they cannot see themselves overweight and dealing with chronic diseases in the future. A company someone works for has a chance of going out of business, but the employee does not work on his resume because he cannot see himself being out of work. In both of these examples, their present and future selves are completely different people.

Being Too Optimistic

Now, being optimistic is not a bad thing; however, getting to the point where you overthink your abilities can be a problem. This is a common occurrence as many people do not work on tasks in the present because they highly believe they can complete it in the future. While this may be true, there will still be an increased amount of stress and anxiety. Also, the potential for oversight and significant errors will be present.

Imagine that you have a 10,000-word paper due to Friday, and it is only Monday. It would make sense to write 1,000-2,000 words daily, instead of waiting until Wednesday or Thursday. When writing the paper ahead of time, you will have extra opportunities to think everything through, and also go back and edit your work. Giving yourself extra time will help you in creating quality work.

Being Indecisive

This is when you cannot make a move because you cannot decide what course of action to take. For example, you may hesitate to apply for a job because you cannot decide which one is best for you. This is a phenomenon known as analysis paralysis, and it has stopped many great people right in their tracks. The following are some factors that make it difficult to make a decision.

- The more options you have, the harder it will be to decide a preferable path to take.
- The more similar different options are, the harder it will be to choose. You might end up analyzing the smallest sectors of each choice.
- The more important the decision is, the harder it will be to make because of the impact it will have on you and others.

It is best if you can keep your decisions to a minimum, as well as your choices. Each time you make a decision, you deplete your mental resources to a degree. So, if you make a host of decisions in a short time period, you have a high likelihood of getting burned out.

Task Aversion

People often procrastinate because they are not looking forward to a task they need to perform. For example, they might have to call them back to resolve a payment dispute but are not looking forward to talking with a customer service representative. As a result, They put off doing it. If you are avoiding a task because of the aversion you have to it, you are just delaying your agony. Imagine how good you will feel after doing it. So, hold your nose and get it done.

Perfectionism

People often want things so perfect that they are terrified of doing something out of fear of the mistakes they will make. Instead of starting and taking their chances, they avoid moving forward. Perfectionism has been called the enemy of productivity because of all the delays it creates along the way. People do not realize that things will no be perfect, so they waste excessive time trying to ake things this way.

Self-Handicapping

Many individuals are terrified of exposing their lack of ability for something. As a result, they procrastinate so they can use it as an excuse for poor performance. They would rather that people think they're lazy than incapable. Procrastinators with this mindset are more likely to put things off if they feel that failure will reflect badly on them.

These are some of the most common reasons for procrastination. There is no easy answer to why people avoid doing things, but it must be overcome for people to start accomplishing things. The following are a few more reasons for procrastination:

- Self-sabotage
- Low self-efficacy
- Perceived lack of self-control
- Fear of being criticized

Sometimes, there are more urgent situations, like ADHD, depression, or low self-esteem, that need to be addressed. The better question to ask is: Why put something off until tomorrow if I can get it done today?

Other Major Reasons for Not Getting Things Done

For some reason, people are just not getting as many things done as they could. Now, I am not saying you have to be on the go all the time. That is not healthy, either. What I am saying is that you need to accomplish things within a certain time period, or you will never achieve anything in life. This will not just affect you, but those who rely on you, as well, like employees, business partners, and family members. To make the world go around, people need to get things done. Yet, they don't. I already spoke about procrastination as a major factor. I will now detail a few other reasons why this happens.

Not Sure What to do

Many people do not do anything because they have no idea what they should do. Even if they have a goal, they are clueless about how to get started in any way. This often occurs because we see other people's accomplishments but have no idea how they achieved them. We keep trying to guess but can't figure it out. Even if we do become aware of how something was accomplished, the values do not line up with our own, which makes us even more confused. It is better to keep on track with your own beliefs when trying to accomplish a goal, rather than rejecting them completely. Rejecting your values will make you even more confused.

There is No Deadline or Accountability

Accountability seems to be going by the wayside these days. People don't get things done because they are not expected to. There is often no disciplinary actions taken, so people continue to lack the drive to move forwards.

Also, when deadlines are nonexistent, then there is no need to get moving. Either we don't create deadlines for ourselves, or other people don't place them on us. If you work for someone and they do not set deadlines, then the operations of the company are not very sound. If you do not set your own deadlines for goals, then you need to start doing so. Make them concrete and not too far out. Remember, you don't want to fall into a procrastination step.

Set a specific date for when you want to accomplish something and stick to it completely. Set it around important events if you can. For example, if you are planning a vacation or will be attending a concert, make it a goal to finish a certain project or reach a specific endpoint. If you are attending a wedding, and you also need to get in shape to fit into your suit, you can make a goal to lose 10 pounds prior to the wedding.

Don't See Any Consequences

This goes along the lines of accountability, but the reason so many people don't get things done is that they do not realize the consequences until they already occur. For example, if your roof needs to be fixed, you will probably put it off because you do not see any consequences for doing so. Of course, on the night that it's pouring rain and the roof suddenly collapses, you will recognize your mistake. Start seeing the potential consequences of not getting things done. Write them down if you have to. Once you see them visually, then you are more likely to take them seriously. For example, if you need new tires on your car and you have been putting it off, then write down that you will get stranded on the freeway with four ruptured tires.

Why Getting Things Done is Critical

Here is the bottom line. The many advancements we have made in this world were done by go-getters who acted constantly. They were not done by people who refused to do the work. As you look back on history, any type of accomplishment, whether good or bad, had massive action behind it. I say bad, as well, because there have been many negative events in our history. I hope you keep your goals positive.

Getting things done creates a sense of accomplishment. No matter how much or how little you do today, it is far better than doing nothing. Nothing gets you nowhere while small steps create some progress.

Getting things done now is the ultimate productivity hack available. There are no tricks or secret formulas. It is simply a matter of doing something now, rather than nothing at all. Whatever you can manage to do within a given period of time, do it, and you will be that much closer.

Imagine having to paint a house. This is not an easy task, especially if you have a big house. Let's say, for this example, the house has 100 walls to paint. If you pain one a day, that is still something. After 100 days, which is just over three months, you will have painted the whole house. Taking three months is better than nothing at all. On certain days, when you have more time and energy, you can paint extra on those days. If painting your house is a goal, then give yourself a deadline with rewards or punishments along the way. For example, if you are not halfway done by a certain date, then cancel something you were looking forward to. Hold yourself accountable, and if you need to, have someone else hold you accountable too.

In the next chapter, I will cover many different tips to start getting things done.

Chapter 2: It's Time to Get Things Done

Now that I have covered the reason why people don't get things done; it is now time to start taking action. This chapter will be focused on various strategies to overcome the blocks in your life. Start following these, and you will be accomplishing things in no time.

Overcoming Procrastination

It's time to stop putting things off. Many of your dreams and goals have gone unfulfilled because you waited too long to start working on them. The world has also missed out on your gifts because you had the potential to create something great if you only took some action in completing it. The following are some ways to overcome one of the greatest obstacles to not getting something done: Procrastination.

Don't Catastrophize

This means that you make a bigger deal out of things than you should. This could be based on the results you might get, or the excruciating the actual task will be. In any event, you are expecting the process to be unbearable.

Here's a little tip: it won't be. We often overthink to the point that our mind creates a scenario that is not conducive to reality. The truth is, hard work, boredom, and other challenges will not kill you. You may not enjoy them on time, but you will overcome them. Also, the results we get are rarely ever at the level we imagine them to be. The thought of a fall is generally harder than the fall itself.

Always believe in yourself that you can make it through something and deal with the consequences, positive or negative, that come with it. The truth is, you can. Even if a task is as horrible as you imagined, you got through it, and it's out of the way. This is much better than thinking about it. Just get it done!

Focus on Your "Why"

You "why" is the ultimate reason for you doing something and should be used as a motivating factor for you. Many procrastinators focus on short-term gains and do not pay attention to long-term potential. This is why it's important to remember your "why." It is the end result you are expecting.

This can be used for any goal in your life, personal or professional. If you have been putting off creating a resume, then imagine yourself in your dream job. If you have been putting off organizing your room, imagine how good you will feel when you can find things easily and don't have to get around a huge mess.

Get Out Your Scheduler

Projects often do not get done because people make no time for them. They will do it when they have time, and therefore, the time will never come. You need to make time and stick to it. Get out your scheduler, whether it's an online planner, paper planner, or calendar, and start blocking off times. Whatever important tasks that need to be completed, write them down and on a specific time and date. Unless something unavoidable comes up, stick to the specific block on your schedule. When people write things down, they are holding themselves accountable. If they miss doing something, they can look at it, and it will remind them.

Be Realistic

Getting things done means you are setting yourself up for success. Do not create unrealistic goals for yourself. Set an achievable goal, and then take specific action steps to get there. For example, do not tell yourself that you will start working out five times a week in the morning immediately when you are not even a morning person. Instead, set up your workout schedule in the evening. If you ultimately want to work out in the mornings, then you can start by doing it once a week and then increasing your days. Do not expect to reach your goals instantly. Set up a long-term plan for success.

Break it Down

Tasks can often become overwhelming, and this leads to procrastination. Break them down into smaller and more manageable tasks with specific deadlines for each small task. If you are planning to landscape your home, start with a small area and give yourself the time you need in each section.

Stop With the Excuses

Here it goes: You will never be fully energized; it will never be the right time; you will often not be in the mood; conditions may never be perfect. Stop using these as excuses. Waiting for any of these will just delay you for no reason. Getting things done is not about waiting for the perfect opportunity. It is about using what you ave to create opportunity. Stop with the excuses!

Find an Accountability Partner

It can be difficult to hold yourself accountable, so find a partner to help you. Express what your goals are to this person and the deadlines that you have. Your accountability partner can then follow up with you and make sure you are staying on track. If you don't reach your deadlines, your partner's job is to grill you as to why. You guys can help each other in this manner to make it a mutual relationship.

Optimize Your Environment

Your environment will play a huge role in creating distractions. Optimize it by finding a quiet place and only having the things you absolutely need. Turn off the TV, social media (I recommend logging out so you can't access it easily), get rid of any papers or clutter that will catch your attention. How many times have you meant to start something, only to get distracted by something else? This is very common, and you must do what you can to avoid it happening to you.

Forgive Yourself

While it might be true that starting something earlier would have been more advantageous, do not beat yourself up for not doing so. You cannot change the past, so forget about it. You can make up for it though by taking advantage of the present. Learn from your past mistake of putting something off and start doing things today. If you should have gone to college five years ago, well, it's okay. You can still go now.

Procrastinators are often trying to avoid distress, but in doing so, they are ironically creating more of it. Start taking the action steps I have described above, and you will no longer be putting things off until tomorrow.

Mindfulness Meditation Technique

Many individuals are not able to get things done because they cannot live in the present moment. They are either anxious about the past or worried about the future. Both of these are unproductive thoughts to have and must be eliminated immediately. You must start focusing on the present, and mindfulness meditation techniques are a great way to do so. Bear in mind, it can take years to master the practice of meditation, so I will just go over the basics to get you started. The following are some structured meditation exercises.

Body Scan Meditation

Start by lying down on your back with your arms at your sides, palms facing up, and legs extended. Now pay close attention and observe every section of your body from head to toe. Become fully aware of any sensations or emotions you are feeling and from where they are coming from. This will bring awareness to yourself and what is happening to you. You will begin living in the present moment with real-time feelings.

Sitting Meditation

Sit in a comfortable position, preferable in a chair, with your back straight, feet flat on the floor, and your palms on your lap. Once in a comfortable position, breathe in slowly through your nose and allow it to go down to your diaphragm.

Then slowly let the breath out. Focus completely on your breathing. If you get distracted by anything, note the experience and then return your attention back to your breathing.

Walking Meditation

Find a quiet space that is at least 15-20 feet in length. Walk slowly between each wall in the room and focus completely on the experience. Be aware of all of the subtle movements that are being used to keep you balanced. Do not pay attention to anything else but your walking.

Simple Mindfulness

The following are a few more mindfulness exercises. These are simple and can be practiced anywhere.

- Focus on your breathing. Take slow and deep breaths in and out. This was done in the meditative position but can also be accomplished standing up anywhere.
- Find joy in the simple pleasures of life and live in the moment.
- Accept yourself and learn to treat yourself like you would a good friend.
- Experience the environment you are in with all of your senses. Do not be in such a rush all the time. Fully taste the food you're eating, stop to

smell the roses, listen to the birds chirping, and even touch some dirt. Feel your surroundings.

15 Habits of Highly Productive People

To become successful, you must mimic the habits of other successful people. The following are effective habits that productive people use every day. These individuals get things done, and you can, as well.

- Focus on the most important tasks first. These are the ones that have the most urgency, the closest deadlines, and the most with the most severe results if not done. Complete them first and then move on to other things.
- Cultivate deep work, which are your hardest, most boring, and most complicated tasks. They have to be done, and if you are not focused fully, they will be missed. Say "no" to people more often, limit distractions, set up a scheduled time for these tasks each day, and go where you do your best work, whether in the office, library, or café, etc.
- Keep a distraction list. While you are working, anytime a distraction comes up, write it down, and then get back to work. This technique works because you are giving attention to your distraction, which eases up its strength over you.

- Use the 80/20 rule. Determine the 20% of your work that requires the most attention. Look at the remaining 80% and see what you can cut out to make more time for the 20%.
- Take scheduled breaks. Even though you want to get a lot done, you cannot just work 24/7. Take scheduled breaks throughout your workday and spend the rest of the time being fully focused. For instance, spend 55 minutes working hard, then take a 10 minutes break to relax and eat something.
- Limit the number of decisions you have to make. Decisions that aren't important should not take up too much of your time or energy. For example, many productive people will wear similar outfits every day because their wardrobe is not as important as other decisions.
- Eliminate insufficient communication. Ignore and delete useless emails, do not engage in too much idle chatter, and avoid gossip, which is a complete waste of time.
- Delegate certain tasks when you can. If you are busy with your career, then you can hire people to do things like take care of your lawn or do your dry cleaning.
- Learn from your successes, as well as your mistakes. Even in success, lessons can be learned about making things more efficient.
- Plan as much as you can for things going wrong because getting caught off guard can be quite a time consumer. It is better to have a plan ahead of time than trying to come up with one urgently.
- Don't wait until you are inspired or motivated to work. Start working and get yourself inspired or motivated.
- Avoid Multitasking. Instead, focus on one task for as long as you can before moving over to the next one.

- Get enough sleep, eat well, exercise, and take time to recharge. This will give you the energy you need when it's time to be productive. Whenever you do something, put all of your effort into it, including rest.
- Take time to get better at tasks by educating yourself and improving your skills.
- Manage your time and energy. Do not waste any of them unnecessarily.

Once you start taking these action steps seriously, you will notice yourself accomplishing a lot more. I will now get into looking towards your future and the life you want to create.

Chapter 3: Visualizing a Better Future

When you learn to get things done and do them well, you will create a better future for yourself. This can become one of your motivations to get moving, as well. In this chapter, I will continue to focus on action steps to get you moving so you can get things done. Once you can visualize your future, you can create it.

How to Visualize Your Future

In this section, I will go over some ways to visualize your future so that you can create an image that inspires you. This is a powerful tool that helps you create the future you want. Will it turn out exactly as you see it? Definitely not. There are too many variables that factor in. However, always keeping that picture in mind means that you will push yourself harder to achieve the success you want. As you see your reality a few years down the line, you will expect more out of yourself. Start by answering the following questions. Remember, these are the answers you hope to give five, 10, 15, or whatever years down the line.

- When someone asks you what you do for work, what do you tell them?
- Describe all of your surroundings in great detail, including your house, the city, neighborhood, and what's nearby. Where do you spend most of your free time?
- What is the atmosphere like at work and in your home, and how do you contribute to it?

- What is your greatest accomplishment? What brings you the most pride?
- Are there any regrets that you have?
- What are the specific steps you took to get where you are?
- What advice would you give to someone else who wants to be where you are?
- What problems arose along the way?

After answering these questions, you will understand where you want to be and have an idea of how to get there.

More Tips for Visualization

Once you begin visualizing your future, then you have it ingrained in your mind. It becomes much harder to let it go. Of course, this does not mean that it's a guarantee. You still must put in the work and make the right moves. For example, if you want to start a business, you can picture the type, how big it will be, where it should be located, how it will look, and whether you plan to have employees or not, among other things. Seeing is believing, though, and the following tips will help you start believing in yourself and your future.

Visualize Your New Life

One way to become excited about your goals is to imagine what your life will be like when you achieve them. For example, if you plan on increasing your salary, imagine that extra money coming in. How much will it be, and what will you be able to do with it? What will you be doing to get that extra money, whether it's through work, investing, or starting a business, etc.? Anything you can imagine about what your life will be like, try to picture it in your mind.

Create a Vision Board

Start collecting images, quotes, articles, and any other visual representations that you feel reflect your future. For instance, you can collect a specific item from a state if you plan on living there someday. This will help you trigger inspiration and hold you accountable for your dreams.

Write Down Your goals

This is a common practice and is touted as being very effective by most productive people. If you are not fond of vision boards, you can write down your goals in lieu of that practice. You may also do it in conjunction with each other for added benefits.

Let Yourself Zone Out

If you find yourself daydreaming at certain times, let it happen. Your mind is trying to tell you something about what you want. Many geniuses in the past, including Einstein, would zone out throughout the day. During these moments, a bolt of inspiration can strike, and great plans can be made. Of course, you cannot daydream all the time, or nothing will get done, which defeats the purpose. However, when you can, take the time to do it.

Say Your Goals Out Loud

Whatever you have planned, whether short-term or long-term, say it out loud, so the universe knows. This also triggers your brain to understand what you want, so it also starts thinking towards that direction.

Think About What You Want and not What You Don't Want

There is a phenomenon known as the Law of Attraction. According to the rules, what you focus on is what the universe delivers to you, even if you're thinking about it in a negative way. So, even if you're thinking about poverty in terms of not falling into it, you will still attract it because it is in your mind. Therefore, it is better not to even visualize poverty but just think about becoming wealthy.

Life When You Get Things Done

All the information and strategies I have gone over in this book lead up to one thing: Getting things done. That is how you achieve what you want in life. You simply must take action and go for what you want. The action steps in the previous chapters provide a way to make goal-getting easier by providing direction, focus, and motivation. I will end this book by over the many benefits of getting things. Getting things done, or GTD is an actual process and state of mind. When you start incorporating it, you will notice many changes during and after.

A Feeling of Relaxed Control

You will feel in control of your life because you are taking active steps to create it. This may be the number one benefit of getting things done. Performing frequent assessments, processing information, and acting on it can make your mind feel like it's water, where it just flows and makes decisions naturally. It takes time for everyone to get to this state.

Your Thinking Will Be Stimulated

When you get things done, your thinking will be stimulated in advance. You will continuously be thinking about the little and big projects in your life, and they will rarely if ever, slip by you. Procrastination will be an afterthought, and you will always be ahead of the curve.

More Organization and Less Clutter

Getting things done means you will clean off your desk literally and figuratively. You will accomplish your tasks and keep your work area organized too. When you get things done, you will be more versatile, and it will become easier to make and keep commitments. In addition, you will be able to keep others accountable for their commitments.

Less Time for Worry

Thinking is good, but overthinking can be detrimental. It can lead to worry, anxiety, and fear. One of the best ways to avoid this is by acting. Worrying occurs when you have a moment for it. When you act, you are doing and have less time to worry.

The entire point of getting things done is just that, getting things done. This is how you accomplish your goals and start living the life you imagine. There are so many get-rich-quick schemes and people promising others the world if they just do a few simple things. With this book, I wanted to provide many different action steps for you so you can tidy up, clear out unnecessary garbage, both emotional and physical, and start working on your dreams. It may take time, but if you're moving in the right direction, that is what matters most.

PART V

Chapter 1: Is This for You?

Before we start this adventure, we have to ask, who is this intended for? The short answer is that it is for everyone who wants to make a positive change in their lives. The key word there is "want". This is ultimately a choice. You must establish your own journey as the techniques exemplified in this book are just practices. There is no set number of meditation sessions that will unlock mindfulness. The practice of these techniques only increases the chances of your own self-discovery. Your willingness to find that goal is the only way these practices will be effective.

This may seem confusing or even overwhelming, but it should be celebrated! You have made a choice to better your life. You possess the bravery to examine yourself in your own state. You are already stronger for it. There is value in yourself and your life and you have already made the decision to discover yourself at your most honest, happiest state and to continue to not only endure but thrive in a world made by your own choices. The biggest step is the first one, and that step is already behind you. It is time to breathe a sigh of relief, to feel accomplished. The worst part of your journey is behind you.

Now that you have made the first step, where do you go? Obviously, the answer is your own choice. The practices in this book are merely there to help you along the way. This may or may not be a path that you have previously gone down, so use these techniques to guide you in your own journey. Look at this book as a toolkit. There is nothing in these pages that will assume a role of authority over you. That is the beauty of free will! You are free to explore at your own pace in your own order.

"Often, it's not about becoming a new person, but becoming the person you were meant to be, and already are, but don't know how to be."

— Heath L. Buckmaster, Box of Hair: A Fairy Tale

You have already made the most important step, and that step is the one that separates you from your furthest setbacks. There is already so much distance between where you were and where you are now. It is now possible to look back and accept yourself. Standing where you are now, it is possible to see your own worth. You are not your setbacks, and you are not your failures. In fact, you might be the most interesting person you know!

Chapter 2: Your Toolbox, DBT

The goal of Dialectical Behavior Therapy (DBT) is to separate you from behaviors that are harmful to yourself and others and replace them with meaningful habits. Now that you have taken your first step and have separated yourself from your setbacks, you can go even further and discover what it is that makes you truly happy on your own. Finding that you do not live to continue harmful behaviors but discovering and tailoring habits that will enhance the life that you are choosing to live will fill you with serenity and self-love, and it will be all the more meaningful because they will be your own interests and not the consequences of your setbacks. Honestly, how exciting is it to really discover the real you? Someone that you may have never met or may not have seen in a long time and neither has anyone else, a brand-new person who has been there all along.

The defined objectives of DBT is obviously a little more clinical. It includes Mindfulness, Distress Tolerance, Interpersonal Effectiveness, and Emotion Regulation. How does this relate to you, though? How do these skills fit into your new and exciting life? Remember that the goal of this kind of therapy is not to overtake your life, but to be there alongside it to help you discover what it is that makes you the real you.

Mindfulness is not a skill set, more so a state of being. Mindfulness is being aware of the present, in the present, and not to be overwhelmed by what is going on around you. It is an awesome way to be and reinforces who you are because only you have a mind like yours. Whenever you are using your senses to become directly aware of your present state of being, you are being mindful. Mindfulness is also exercised like a muscle. It is something that we all possess, but few regularly practice. Although that statement may not be true for long. There is a growing interest in meditation and a growing awareness of the importance of remaining mindful in every aspect of life from personal to even business. If you were to practice it, you will discover that the feeling of mindfulness becomes stronger the more you exercise that mental muscle. Focus and personal honesty will become stronger as you develop along this path. It is an exciting tool of self-discovery and one that will be explored upon later in this book.

Distress Tolerance is a measurement. It is your ability to accept distress that cannot be changed. Emotional pain is measured on a different scale altogether from physical pain, but it can be just as, or even more, damaging. The real skill here is learning how to find your own way around the distress and accept what you are unable to change. Practicing mindfulness will help you to separate yourself from distress factors but coming to terms with the reality of these stressful situations will no longer be a roadblock, but a defining challenge that will make you stronger and give you skills for future distress management.

"Grant me the serenity, to accept the things I cannot change; courage to change the things I can; and wisdom to know the difference."

Learning the difference between what you can and cannot control is paramount. Once you have accepted the reality of a stressful situation that you cannot control, you cease to try to change it but begin to find a path to live around or through it. Sometimes, the energy spent trying to change an unchangeable situation is more stressful than the original event! You owe it to yourself to not harm yourself. There are even times when the situation only seems to be so stressful because you have spent all of your energy and effort trying to change it instead of taking a step back and accepting it for what it is. You could even come to realize that the situation is more benign than how you have built it up to be inside your head. Sometimes, you can even find a way to turn it into a positive situation! You will never be able to do any of that if you are too busy stressing about the original situation, though.

Interpersonal Effectiveness will help you to build and maintain important relationships, including the one you have with yourself, as well as help you to define priorities and to arrange them in a sensible manner to live your new life the most effective. The clinical method is through the acronym DEAR MAN:

- **D**escribe the current situations
- **E**xpress your feelings and opinions
- **A**ssert yourself by asking for what you want, or by saying no
- **R**eward the person – let them know what they will get out of it
- **M**indful of objectives without distractions (attack the problem, not the person)
- **A**ppear effective and competent
- **N**egotiate alternative solutions

These are effective and healthy steps for conflict resolution and a great tool to have in mind to keep your communication on track and working towards an agreeable solution.

Respect is a trait valued by everybody in one way or another. Respect is earned and kept and can encourage stronger relationships with the important people in your life. Speaking in a respectful tone will lead you to your interpersonal goals in a way than getting agitated towards that person, situation, or even yourself. Self-respect is the true basis of interpersonal respect. Have you ever heard that you must learn to love yourself before you can love another? This is because you define for yourself, and exemplify to others, what respect means to you. How you treat yourself will set the standard for how others will feel that they can treat you. A person who dresses nice and speaks warmly with peers will garner more respect than a person who shows little care for how they want to be treated. Self-respect is important, and you deserve it! You are already stronger for having taken this journey and your story is one that no one else has. You are worthwhile, interesting, and unique. Taking good care of yourself will tell others that you are a person who warrants respect. Another acronym that is helpful about self-respect is FAST.

- **F**air to myself and others
- No **A**pologies for being alive
- **S**tick to values (do not do anything you will regret later)
- **T**ruthful without excuses or exaggeration

You have heard the Golden Rule; treat others as you would like to be treated yourself. Well, that rule works the other way as well! Treat yourself as you would treat others. You deserve the same respect that you would show to others, so do not count yourself out or make sacrifices that make you feel uncomfortable. Be fair to yourself!

If you find that you apologize unnecessarily, stop it! Sometimes, people will tell you that you apologize too much, which only make you feel uncomfortable. You do not have to apologize for anything that you are not truly sorry for. You occupy the same space as your peers and you deserve the same level of respect.

What are your values? Do you know? In your current stage of rebuilding and discovery, your values may change, or you may discover that you have been violating your own values for a long time. With a renewed respect for yourself and a bright new path ahead of you, you are most likely to find out what is truly important to you. Find your core values and remember that you deserve respect. You do not have to apologize for your values and you do not have to compromise your values. Make your identity known and remember that you are valid.

Once you know who you are, what you value, and the fact that you deserve and possess self-respect, honesty becomes easy. You do not have to fabricate yourself to fit in or hide any unsavory traits that you may think that you possess. Your peers will respect an honest you. Honesty to yourself and others is the pinnacle of freedom. You are who you are and who you are is a strong, healthy, and an interesting person! Half-truths and flat out lies do little more than create stress for everyone involved, including yourself. A person with self-respect does not need to create an identity that they do not own. Breathe and relax because you are you!

Chapter 3: Finding Yourself through Mindfulness

Discovering yourself is exciting! It's a journey that is enviable. We have already defined mindfulness, so the next step is to discover how it is practiced and define what your individual goals are. It is important to remember to constantly ask yourself what you want to find in this book. Your individual goals are the goals of this text. What practitioners of mindfulness usually find is greater fulfillment, a deeper understanding of their selves, positive behavioral changes, and more importantly, less suffering.

As you continue down this path, it is important to remember what your truest intentions are because doubts will surface. Mindfulness will need to be practiced and exercised like a muscle. Minds are messy, prone to wandering, prone to doubt, and everyone examines themselves much harsher than their peers would. In the last chapter, you discovered what your values are and who you are as a person. You discovered that self-respect is worth having. Now, it is time to reinforce what you know about yourself and what you want to explore.

Before we get to the actual practices, it is important to note that the path to mindfulness is not linear. It is a little different for everyone and the only outside guide is a collection of experiences from others. The true guide is yourself. Do not fret. Do not succumb to doubt because you may or may not discover a path differently or find a truth not listed in this book. No one can know you as well as you can. Instead of reveling in the doubt or confusion, be excited! You are the first to discover your exact path and you are the first to find your own unique solutions to your setbacks.

At the same time, you may discover that these goals are even connected! As you discover greater fulfillment, you may connect it to lesser suffering, and from there, you may find that you exhibit better behavior and more success in your relationships. Understand that practicing separateness from your suffering could lead to accepting validation from your own positive thoughts and energy.

The most obvious exercise for practicing mindfulness is meditation. It is important to note that meditation is not passive. It is not simply sitting and relaxing with your eyes closed. It is an active exploration of your mind while providing yourself with the least resistance to your own self-discovery. You may not just drop right into it during your first session. An unpracticed mind has never explored in that way. You may not know how to look inward as your senses and instincts are conditioned to look outward for stimulation.

First, you must separate yourself from your reactions. You must understand what your automatic reactions to a stimulus such as stress and joy are and be aware of yourself at the moment that you act automatically. You are not your feelings. You are not your reactions. Imagine you are on the side of a road watching traffic pass back and forth. Every car is a stimulus, feeling, or reaction. You are separate from them and you must merely make a mental note of it, and then let it pass. Be aware of their existence and acknowledge them, but do not react to them. Eventually, your mind will become more still.

Another example is to imagine your mind like a still pool of water. Every thought and stimulus is a pebble dropped in that pool. Those pebbles create concentric ripples that expand outward, and then even out. If you reach into the water to grab that pebble, you will only create a splash and larger ripples. Eventually, the pebbles will slow, and your quietest realizations and truths will surface. Do not fear! This is your truest self. This is exciting and another great achievement along with your journey to a more peaceful and successful you. After those truths have passed without judgment, your pool of water will fall even more still. You will experience true serenity and discover the most honest definition of a quiet mind. This is peace.

To practice meditation, you must first dedicate time and space to your session. You do not need a special pillow or certain music or any equipment whatsoever, just time and space to practice. Sit in a comfortable position that you will not stress to maintain and close your eyes. Next, just acknowledge the moment as it is. Observe it without judgment or interaction. Just simply be in the moment without exerting effort or energy towards it. Pay attention to the sensations of air passing through your nostrils or the presence of sound in your ears. Let the moment pass through you as you sit peacefully in it. The goal is not simply to be calm, it is to be aware of the moment as it is happening right now without interaction or judgment. The next step is not so much a step, but a reassurance. Judgments will rise. It is inevitable, especially when you are first practicing. Remain calm and remain practicing. Do not succumb to doubt or frustration. Simply make a note of it, and let it pass. This is an excellent practice for learning how to move on from frustration or feelings of grudge in your waking life. If your mind wanders too far off of your initial concentration, keep returning to the sensation of your breath. Focus on the gentle sensation of the in and out of your breathing. Simply be in your awareness.

Meditation is a proven method to reduce stress, increase clarity, and can even positively rearrange your brain chemistry! You will notice your brain will have less chatter in your normal life, and you will be less prone to anxiety. It is a great practice for finding a "third way" around a conflict. It can even open up your creativity and lower your heart rate and blood pressure. As I have mentioned before, it has even begun to appear in modern business practices. Some higher up CEOs have adopted this daily practice to increase their creativity and productivity and reduce their stress level in the fast-paced environment that is business. Everyone from athletes to political figures to your average working man benefits from this simple practice.

If you chose to partake in this particular practice, you are unlikely to regret it. The next chapter will focus on advanced meditation techniques for when you discover that you like this new calmer, more focused you!

Chapter 4: Taking Mindfulness to the Next Level with Advanced Meditation Techniques

If you have chosen to give meditation a try, then congratulations! You should feel proud of yourself for having the courage to try something new. You should feel reinforced in your feelings of solidity in your new and healthy life. You have made an actual effort and have taken real-life actions! This is another moment to look at just how far you have come. How has meditation affected your life already? Do you feel a renewed clarity? This chapter will show you advanced techniques that you can practice to further expand your meditation practices.

An easy form of meditation that you can incorporate in your daily life is called a Walking Meditation. Obviously, this can be done simply while walking, or any form of ambulation that you use to get around. It is an action that you do naturally and has been for years. You probably learned how to walk before you learned how to read! This kind of easy, almost automatic and steady movement is a perfect environment to study your meditation practices.

First, you must stand up straight. Keep your back straight as you practice this. It is important to find the posture that is comfortable and promotes easy steps and focus. Next, place your hands together just above your belly button with your thumbs curled in towards your palms. This position promotes a comfortable posture that brings your focus to your center. Your arms are not swaying, and you feel self-contained and comfortable. Now, let your gaze drop slightly. This will also allow you to focus while being aware of where you are walking to. Just like with normal sitting meditation, try not to get lost in outside stimuli, just simply make a note of them and continue on with your focus inwards. Now, you are ready to take your first step. In the last section, I mentioned that breathing could be used to bring your focus back to your center. In this exercise, you will use your steady footfalls to create a rhythmic cadence for you to keep your central focus on. Notice, without interacting, the sensation of the ground on your feet (or whatever mode of transportation that you would use to get around on your own). Notice as the ground rolls from the back to the front of your foot. Notice the gentle bounce of your body as you move along. Now, do the same with the next step and the next. Make sure to walk at a slightly slower pace than usual. It is not necessary to move ridiculously slow, just make sure that it is at a pace where you are able to focus on your gentle and rhythmic movements and still move along at a comfortable speed.

Benefits of this style of meditation are that it allows you to further exercise your focus outside of the room or environment that you have become comfortable meditating in. It allows you to start connecting that focus to your daily life as you practice maintaining that focus during the natural and unpredictable distractions that occur just in a day out. You will also begin to appreciate the seemingly mundane aspects of your day, bringing focus and renewed eyes to aspects of this wonderful life that may have gone unnoticed or underappreciated previously. A cloud moving in front of the sun might bring certain effects to your attention like the changing colors or temperature of this temporary state. You might find a renewed appreciation for the sun and life in general. A gentle breeze might remind you of how temporary forces in your life are. A passing conversation might show you how calm, focused, and centered you are feeling in the moment versus how frantic and anxious the average person is in their daily life. You will discover all of these things while keeping your focus centered. It is important to not react to any of their thoughts, just simply recognize the existence of these thoughts, and let them pass naturally on their own. Bringing your meditation practices from your sterile environment to the waking world is an excellent practice for learning how to maintain and call upon this state of focus when there are events in your life that may be exciting or stressful.

The next technique is quite the opposite. Instead of walking, this technique is most effective while laying down, but it can be done in a sitting position. It is called a Body Scan, and it is used to focus on your physical wellbeing. It gives the sensation of infusing your body with a healing breath.

First, you must sit or lie in a comfortable position. Do not pick a position or surface that will become uncomfortable or distracting during your meditation. Once you are in a good position, place your hands on your stomach in the same manner in which you did during the Walking Meditation, just above your belly button in a comfortable position that brings your focus to the center of your body in a full rest. Once you are in this position, you might find it easier to focus if you close your eyes. Now, take a few deep breaths. Take note of the moment as you are in it, just like you have practiced in the basic meditation technique. Then bring your attention to your body. Notice the sensation and pressure of the floor or chair on your back or legs. Keep taking deep breaths, but this time, notice the invigorating life that fills your body when you inhale deeply and then feel a deeper sense of relaxation on every exhale. Fall deeper and deeper into your focused state with each incremental breath. You may start to notice more minute sensations such as your pulse under your skin, or little hairs standing up on your arm as your body becomes more relaxed and focus.

Now, bring your focus to your stomach area. If your stomach is tense, let it loose. You might even notice that your entire body relaxes as you release the tension in your stomach. Shift your focus from your stomach to your hands just above that area. See if you can allow your hands to soften even more. Feel your body relax even another level. Now, bring your focus to your arms. Let the tension loose in your shoulders. Let the tension loose in your biceps and forearms. After that, it is time to bring your focus to your neck. Let the muscles in your neck relax. It is perfectly acceptable to let your body shift as your muscles become systematically more relaxed. It is almost bound to happen as you are achieving new levels of relaxation. How relaxed you are now will make your initial assessment when you first lied down seem so distant.

After you have relaxed your neck, then it is time to focus on your jaw. Let that tension go. In your waking life, the average person carries extra tension especially in their jaw, shoulders, and fists without even realizing it. You might perceive yourself as relaxed when in actuality; you are much tenser than what is comfortable. This is one of those realizations that you come across through meditation that is an invaluable lesson that you have taught yourself. After you have rolled your relaxing focus over your entire body, take a mental snapshot of your body as a whole. Notice your body in the same way that you notice passing thoughts in the basic meditation technique. You may realize that your body is yours, but it is not you. Your body is a vessel and a tool for who you really are. That separation is important when you practice meditation. It is what allows you to examine thoughts without attachment. Take one more deep breath and allow your eyes to open, feeling a new sense of invigoration and relaxation.

Congratulations! With these three meditation techniques; the basic meditation, the Body Scan, and the Walking Meditation, you are able to perceive and react to thoughts and stimuli within your mind, your body, and your world in a healthy way. There is nothing that you should not be able to process using these techniques. You now have the tools to tackle any hardships along your journey. On top of that, you now have a new perspective that is exciting to explore as you find new hobbies, relationships, and life choices. Now even simple tasks like breathing, walking, or even just existing can be healing and full of positive energy!

The next chapter will focus on processing negative thought patterns in a healthy way. Now that you have this new perspective and new tools, it should be easy to separate yourself from negative thoughts that may surface from your past or present life. Do not fear! You are ready. You are stronger than you have ever been, and you can tackle any setbacks you have experienced, or are currently experiencing. Take a moment to celebrate where you are versus where you have been!

Chapter 5: Using Your New Tools to Process Negative Emotions

Negative emotions will occur. It is the inevitability that comes with the endless possibilities of life. You cannot reasonably expect to live your entire life and never feel sad, hurt, angry, betrayed, embarrassed, or any other emotion that can be perceived as negative. In this chapter, we will review the skills that you have learned to more effectively process your emotions when an inevitably negative emotion occurs. Through Dialectical Behavior Therapy, Emotion Regulation breaks down into three goals.

1. Understand one's emotions
2. Reduce emotional vulnerability
3. Decrease emotional suffering

The first step begins with a simple truth, and that is emotions are not bad. Even negative emotions are not something to just be avoided. It is impossible, and unhealthy to attempt, to avoid every negative emotion that you will come across in your life. Attachment to negative feelings is what causes real suffering. You learned from the last two chapters how to separate yourself from thoughts and emotions. You simply must acknowledge the emotion and/or event, and then let it pass. It is important to acknowledge these emotions, though. Try to define your emotions clearly. Using phrases like "I feel bad" does not give a clear understanding of how you are feeling. Instead of "bad", expand on that. Pinpoint it by saying you feel frustrated, depressed, anxious, or angry. Understanding what and how you are feeling is integral to processing those feelings. It is also important to understand the difference between primary and secondary emotions.

Primary emotions are reactions to an outside stimulus, and secondary emotions are reactions to those primary emotions. For example, if you felt depressed later about being too angry at a friend, then anger would be the primary emotion while depression would be the secondary emotion. The secondary emotion is a judgment of the primary emotion. Learning how to acknowledge emotions without judgment is essential because secondary emotions are destructive. Also, learning how to process negative events without succumbing to negative emotions is very important. Maybe being angry at the friend was not the proper response when you could have used the DEAR MAN acronym in the second chapter of this book to properly resolve that event and those feelings in a way that would solve the issue and be beneficial to both you and your friend. Remember that emotions are not your identity. Emotions are there just to alert you to stimuli that are beneficial or problematic. How you process and express these emotions is entirely up to you.

Reducing emotional vulnerability will increase the stability of your emotions, simply put. In DBT, the methods for reducing emotional vulnerability is through action. It will teach you to create positive habits and experiences to balance out the negative feelings you might be feeling. An easy acronym to remember for this is PLEASE MASTER.

PL – represents taking care of your physical body and reducing or treating illness
E – eat a balanced diet
A – is for avoiding alcohol and drugs, which can only heighten or fabricate negative feelings
S – Sleep. It is important to get regular sleep
E – The last E is for exercise. Much like meditation, it will increase in benefits the more you practice.
MASTER – This one is the fun one. Master positive activities to increase your sense of well-being and accomplishment.

Your health affects your emotional state. This ties into the self-respect section that we talked about in the second chapter. You will feel much better physically and emotionally if you raise your standards of how you treat yourself. Getting regular sleep, exercise, and only treating your body and yourself to healthy food and activities will do absolute wonders for your confidence. This also includes avoiding alcohol and drugs. It is too easy to mask feelings with these substances, and as we have learned, that is not a healthy way to process those emotions. Avoiding emotions, especially with mind-altering substances, does not make those emotions go away. It is not a permanent solution, it only encourages you to chase that perceived temporary safety from those emotions while your body is developing an addiction to the actual substance. It is a trap and can only work to undo all of the work that you have already accomplished. Treat yourself better than that because not only do you have self-respect, but you deserve it.

Now, I am going to circle back to the PL portion of the PLEASE MASTER acronym. After you understand the steps necessary for taking care of your body, you will understand that it is important to monitor your body as a whole. This includes taking care of illnesses when they arrive. Illness is another inevitability of life. Much like emotions, it is important to process them in a healthy manner to avoid further damage. You deserve to live in a healthy body and you owe it to yourself to take care of yourself. Living in a healthy body will give you peace of mind. Knowing that at the end of the day, you are physically feeling healthy will put other situations in perspective and it will be one more positive that you can weigh against negative emotions when they occur. Along with exercise and meditation, you can choose to MASTER other positive activities in your life. Developing or rediscovering a hobby is exciting and can give new meaning and a new sense of accomplishment in your life!

After you have learned these skills, you are ready to learn how to decrease emotional suffering. In DBT, it is comprised of only two skills: Letting go and taking opposite action.

Letting go refers to what we have already learned, by using our mindfulness to process emotions in a healthy way by letting them pass without developing secondary emotions to attach to the primary emotions. Taking opposite action means engaging in actions that are in direct contrast to the negative feelings that you are experiencing. For example, instead of crying when a feeling of depression is acknowledged, try to stand straight, speak confidently, and react to the stimulus or event in a healthy way. This is not to ignore that emotion. It is an exercise to lessen the length and severity of the emotion. It is important to acknowledge emotions, but that does not mean that you have to be subordinate to them. You do not need to let emotions control how you think and act. It can also give you a new perspective on a situation that you may have reacted automatically too.

With these skills, coupled with the skills you have learned in the previous few chapters, you can process emotions internally in your mind, body, and everyday life and also express those emotions after you have processed them. Even more to add to that, you have developed a renewed sense of self-respect through self-care and new or rediscovered hobbies. You are now taking steps to replace negative habits and feelings with positive feelings and activities you enjoy and that are uniquely representative of you! You may start to feel that you are meeting the real you, a more positive and honest version of yourself, doing things that you enjoy.

Chapter 6: Defining Your Goals, Your Values, and Yourself

Now, instead of learning something new, it is time to reassess yourself after what you have already learned. Do you remember those goals and values that you defined for yourself at the beginning of this book? Well much like how we discovered new levels of relaxation during the Body Scan meditation, it is time to discover new levels of yourself. Maybe after you have practiced meditation and studied the different goals of DBT, your renewed sense of self and awareness can further sharpen your goals and expectations from your new life. It is even possible that you have already achieved and mastered some of your goals. If you have, then congratulations! It is time to reassess what is important to you and what you can get out of this book. If you have not achieved any of your goals yet, then do not worry! Hopefully, you have set expectations at a reasonable level and you are mindful of what you are able to achieve within yourself. It is good to have both long-term and short-term goals. It is important, even, to balance both so you are able to celebrate achievements along the path to a life-affirming goal that you may not have been able to achieve without taking that all important first step along this journey.

Each new skill you learn is a skill you would not have had if you would have maintained your negative feelings and habits. There are questions for you now that only you can answer. How is it that you feel? How do you feel in a general sense of wellbeing? How far along do you think you have traveled? You are most likely aware of your progress and it is good to celebrate along the way. These steps you are taking are not steps that any one person could take for you, no matter how influential or qualified. Just like how meditation and mindfulness is a study of you, the steps you have taken are entirely unique to you.

Having said all of that, it is important to allow positive feelings to be acknowledged and witnessed. Many have a hard time accepting themselves in their own achievements. Judgments upon oneself can absolutely be the harshest. It is easy for faults and negative feelings to seem large and overwhelming when you are standing so near to them. These negative feelings cause you to stress and can be impossible to simply ignore. This is why we learn to process those feelings and resolve them instead of trying in vain to ignore them. An unresolved negative feeling can trigger a survival response, which is why it is impossible to ignore said feelings. In this way, unresolved negative feelings make it near impossible to accept positive feelings about yourself.

Your body does not feel the need to react to positive feelings because it feels that the situation is resolved because it ended on a satisfying conclusion. Your body will tell you that your time and effort need to be spent resolving those negative feelings because they are triggering a survival response in you. Now that you have learned how to bring negative feelings to a positive and productive conclusion, it is now possible to accept your positive traits and individuality. It is even possible to meet yourself without those impossible stresses in your life. How exciting and life-affirming is that! How much better off are you now in relation to how you were before you took this journey?

Now, that you know your goals, and you know yourself, what are your values in your new life now? What have you learned that you could possibly maintain, or even teach others? Maybe you recognize the work that you have put in and are starting to recognize the results of hard work. Maybe you value patience and understanding because practicing meditation has taught you how to discover feelings that were always there, just buried. All this book can do is speculate and give examples to what you may be feeling. It is your unique journey that is your real teacher. You have taught yourself how to heal. You have taught yourself how to take the first step, and you have taught yourself how to recognize greatness within yourself.

Are there people in your life who would be proud of you for where you are now? If so, you should greet them and share your renewed sense of pride and clarity with them. It is reaffirming of your own sense of accomplishments to have it validated by those you love, those you admire, and those you respect. Sometimes, it can give a new perspective to emphasize with someone else and share a joyful feeling with them. You are no longer in a cave of your own misjudgments, both internal and external. You have established yourself out in the light. You can walk among the world with your head high instead of living in the past and inside of your own head. You see the world for how it actually is and not through the lens of prior transgressions or feelings of worthlessness. It is even possible to look back at how you used to exist and treat yourself and separate yourself enough from it that you can even brush it off. That is not you anymore. You are the real you now. You are the you that you were meant to be, a much happier and more honest you who recognizes real emotions instead of perceived injustices to yourself.

Chapter 7: Living in the Positive!

Now that you have created a positive atmosphere for your mind to exist in, you are probably feeling a new motivation and longing to explore the world in your new self. What do you do with all of this motivation? It is important to put this good energy to use as to not fall back into negative habits that your old self has come to reinforce. You are at a crucial step where you should give great importance to channeling this positive energy into positive habits.

Something that you can do for yourself is to continue to practice meditation and exercise. Your new positive life starts at your core. Your core being yourself. You have learned a renewed sense of self-respect and discovered some deep insight into yourself. Now, it is time to maintain it. You can continue to live positive as long as you take care of yourself. Imagine yourself in a fancy car. It can look nice on the outside, but if the engine is not kept in good condition, it will not function as intended. Every new positive action starts with a sense of wellbeing.

Other ways to maintain your emotional stability through practice is to find a creative outlet for your feelings. If you feel that you are the creative type of person, then you may already have some of these hobbies. You may even have hobbies that you have not visited in a long time. Picking up an old hobby can help you connect with who you were before you found yourself down a darker path. It can give you a sense that you are picking up where you left off and reassure you that this you is the real you. If you are not a creative person or have not found an interest in a hobby, then do not worry! Another way that you can strengthen your mental focus and reinforce this new positive you are to learn. Reading is a proven method to increase cognitive faculties and helps you to directly discover interesting perspectives that you may not have come to on your own independently. Maybe, you will even discover ways to learn about aspects of your life that you have put on hold. Projects and promises made to others and you can now be fulfilled because you are now breathing easy and have a new motivation for life.

Great! Now that you have a healthy and positive sense of wellbeing, you can further reinforce your new positive life by engaging in productive social activities. Before I get into examples of this, I want to further explore the benefits.

Giving back to your community outwardly shows that you want to be engaged with society. You recognize yourself as a part of a whole and you are devoid of an ego that alienates you from your peers. It is not a struggle for your individuality though; you have already explored and defined yourself to yourself. Now, it is time to show who you are to the world! A person who lives inside of their own negative thought patterns does not want to be a part of society. They will build their own mental walls to keep themselves from embarrassment, anger, shame, or any other negative thought patterns associated with social interaction. Maybe they feel that society owes them something. An overinflated ego is another trepidation to avoid. Now that you are free of all of these negative thought patterns, you can enjoy social interaction with a head held high and nothing to apologize for. Another key benefit that you may not have seen or realized before, is that doing something nice for others simply feels good. You are able to emphasize the happiness of others. Seeing a smile on another person's face that you have caused can feel so rewarding in ways that you have never felt before! Even for more selfish reasons, it feels good, as in the sense of being the hero of someone's day. It is a wholesome feeling. It is a feeling that is entirely guilt-free. Some examples of positive social outings would be simple activities like volunteer work or attending or even participating in sports events. Maybe your place of employment has a softball league, or your colleagues enjoy disc golf. These are activities that directly give back to your community or peer group. These are higher levels of commitment, so if you are not ready for that quite yet, maybe you could try something a little less structured. Meeting trusted friends in a relaxed social environment could be a little bit more comfortable for you. Invite a friend, or a few friends, out for lunch or to a store of your common interests. This kind of setting makes for a good conversation that is not so personal if you are not ready for that. It is perfectly acceptable to take your time developing your social identity, as this step is very important. Meeting friends in this kind of setting can also help you learn more about your friends and even yourself! Maybe they have an interest that you did not even know that you had! Maybe you have a friend who is very interested in tabletop gaming, which might be an area of interest that you have never explored! Your friends and new interests will most likely lead you to new friends and even more positive and interesting activities. It is easy to get sucked into the positive life; all you have to do is take the first step!

Working within your comfortable level of commitment is essential, but it is also important to actually engage in these or similar activities. The goal of this section is to establish new positive habits to replace self-destructive habits. Just like how picking up and reading this book was a crucial first step, this is another crucial step. Do not fret though! This step is easier than what you would think. Most of the time, the fear associated with the activity is much worse than the actual activity, and you should know how to properly process negative thought patterns. All you have to do is breathe and take that step. Your friends, family, and colleagues will be more than happy to have you included.

It is important to establish positive relationships that engage in positive activities. It is also important to allow yourself to learn what positive social activities are. A common misconception, reinforced by advertisements and common television shows, is that all social activity takes place with alcohol. That is simply not true. In fact, the most productive and happiest people may rarely step foot in one of these establishments. As a side note, you may also be surprised at the money you save when you do not frequently visit these establishments, which brings me back to advertisements. That is why those media outlets pursue that lifestyle; it is purely to promote a lifestyle that will earn their company more money. In that respect, establish your own idea of happiness! Find out what it is that truly makes you happy! You are most likely to find that engaging with friends develops real bonds and promotes honest happiness. You are most likely to find that volunteer work, or even saying yes when someone asks for a favor, is more fulfilling than anything that you have experienced in your previous life.

You should feel proud of yourself for taking this step! Now that you are taking steps to not only better yourself, but to solidify and reinforce it with positive social activities, there is nothing that can get in your way on your path to being happier, more wholesome you! Once again, congratulations!

Chapter 8: How DBT Has Enhanced Your Life

Although this book has seemed to have an almost conversational flow, it has actually followed very closely to the five functions of DBT. As this book has mentioned before, the goal of this is not to assume an authoritative role over you, the reader. This book was designed to reinforce your own choices and merely give examples of positive living for those who may be unaware or fearful of how to live as such. Having said that, it is now time to relate what we have learned to the five functions of Dialectical Behavior Therapy. Before we do that, let's define what those five functions are.

- Enhance client's capabilities
- Improve the client's motivation
- Assure generalization to the client's natural environment
- Structure the environment
- Enhance the therapist's capabilities and support their motivation

The clinical way to go about enhancing your capabilities is to reinforce the skills of DBT. We have used many skills directly from the actual standard of DBT, such as the acronyms DEAR MAN, FAST, and PLEASE MASTER. These are acronyms that you would become familiar with if you were to attend a regular DBT session. We have also discussed important skills like practicing mindfulness and emotional regulation. These are also skills that you are most likely to encounter in an actual DBT session. This book has taken those lessons and broken them down for you to study, practice, and make into your own at your own pace by your own choices. Using these skills in your own life will only work to enhance the quality of your life and introduce you to lifestyles that mirror your interests, even those that you may not be aware that you have. This is an exciting time to be alive, and an exciting time for you!

The next function of DBT is the enhancement of the client's motivation. This book was designed to keep you motivated throughout, but it is not what was written or the speed in which you read it. The real motivation comes from you. You have rewarded yourself for picking up this book and sticking to it all the way to the end. By now, you deserve to have developed a sense of pride in making these positive changes in your life! There is no outside force that can motivate you to the extent that you can motivate yourself.

This book was written to be a companion to your own life. You are free to read or not read, follow or not follow, at your own pace. The fact that you have made it this far is something to be celebrated. It shows that you are honest in your desire to rid yourself of negative thought processes and self-destructive habits. There is not a single person or entity that is able to instill that level of motivation inside of you. You have shown that you are committed; not to this book or these processes, but you are committed to yourself. You have already taken better care of yourself than previously you might have thought possible. It is not only acceptable but appropriate to celebrate yourself at this time. This is a real achievement that you have accomplished, and one that many people take multiple tries to achieve. Some may not ever get to the level of clarity and health that you have already achieved for yourself. Once again, Congratulations!

The third function of DBT may seem confusing at first. It is to assure generalization to the client's natural environment. What that means is that this treatment, and this book, is designed to be a companion piece to live alongside without overtaking your life. This is not a program designed to put your life on hold. The effectiveness of this is that it promotes ease of transition into your new lifestyle while giving examples that are digestible by you because they relate to you, just as you are. It is easy to take this book with you and read it at your own pace or use the skills you have learned through a DBT session or in this book while you go about living your day-to-day life. There is no commitment besides the commitment that you have made to yourself and are comfortable with.

In an actual DBT session, they would address this function within the moment coaching. You would have access to a 24/7 phone number that you would be encouraged to call if you are having a hard time with applying the lessons to your life you would have learned during a session. This is an excellent tool, and if you were to attend a DBT session, I would strongly encourage you to feel free to use it. These coaches are not there to judge your choices. They understand the material and are also encouraged to process emotions without judgment. This is purely for the benefit of you! It is also encouraging to have outside motivation when your motivation might be hitting a low point. There is nothing to worry about though, just like the inevitability of sickness or negative thoughts, you cannot fault yourself for when your motivation is feeling weaker at the moment. Just relax, call that number, and celebrate yourself for making the positive choice at that moment when you may not have previously.

We are almost through the list here, I hope that you feel encouraged to continue. The fourth function of DBT is to structure the client's environment. This one can seem almost scary because you have gone this far along your own choices. There is nothing to fear though because this step is not designed to take away your choices, merely to help you and provide tools for you to make positive choices when you may not have previously. How a DBT session would go about doing that would be to assign you a case manager. This is someone who is dedicated to your case and is working with you to ensure your success.

An important aspect of this function is the thought process when accepting it. It is not there to control your lifestyle. When a client has made poor life choices and made a habit out of them, then they might not be aware of or be comfortable with lifestyle choices that are more positive and sustainable. You have already decided to live a positive life, now it is time to learn how. That is the purpose of this function. In DBT, there is a strong focus on replacing negative habits with more positive habits. This is because pure motivation has to be outwardly expressed and used for it to continue. Imagine your positive motivation as a match. You can light the match, and it will burn for a while. It is hot, it is bright. It has the potential to continue on, but it can only continue on if fuel is introduced to the match. Imagine this function of DBT as a pile of wood arranged for you in a fire pit, ready to be lit by your motivational match. Once you apply the match to the wood in the fire pit, then the fire burns much longer in a safe environment. Your motivation must be applied to a positive atmosphere to continue on. Your case manager or other individuals in your DBT session use this function to safely provide you with those structured, positive environments. Go forth and do well for yourself and others!

Have you made it this far? I hope that you have because this is now the final function of Dialectical Behavior Therapy. That function is to enhance the therapist's capabilities and support their motivation. DBT therapists work in a team to more effectively enhance the lives and understanding of their clients. This is important for the team as well as the client. A typical DBT team meeting may start with a mindfulness exercise, reading of the previous minutes, and then discuss strategies to further their treatment. It is important for you to be engaging and helpful along with your therapist as this whole treatment only works with your commitment. An example of this would be to imagine you and your therapist on a rowboat. Your therapist will not be able to motivate you to continue to row if they are not participating in the work. Your therapist can also not row by themselves if you are not helping. This whole style of treatment is designed to be a cooperative endeavor. You should feel excited and encouraged to participate. The end result will be a happier, more positive you!

This chapter is here to serve the purpose of relating what you have learned to the structured skills that are discussed in an actual Dialectical Behavior Therapy session. It is strongly encouraged that you attend these sessions and take what you have learned in this book with you to those sessions. There is nothing that you should not be able to achieve in this aspect of your life between this book, those sessions, and your own motivation! You have a threefold angle of attack on your negative habits that you wish to eradicate from your life. Finding a DBT session is easy, as it is a growing style of treatment. Everyone involved wishes only the best of success for you! Continue on with your own choices and feel proud of how far you have come!

www.ingramcontent.com/pod-product-compliance
Lightning Source LLC
Chambersburg PA
CBHW071733080526
44588CB00013B/2009